MEANWHILE, HERE IN AUSTIN
Copyright 2025 Cetywa Powell
All Rights Reserved
Published by Underground Voices
Third edition paperback

Underground Voices
www.undergroundvoices.com
uveditor@undergroundvoices.com

Cover Design: Cetywa Powell
ISBN: 978-0-9988923-7-5

This is a love letter to you.
To you, Austin.
Because you led me here and welcomed me
in that warm, Southern way.
And I knew... as I'll tell you again later...
I knew that I would be happy here.

You're not perfect.
Is any city?
Your winters are erratic, and your summers - well.
But you have brought me a peace of mind that few cities have.
And for that reason,
I will always be grateful.

Spring

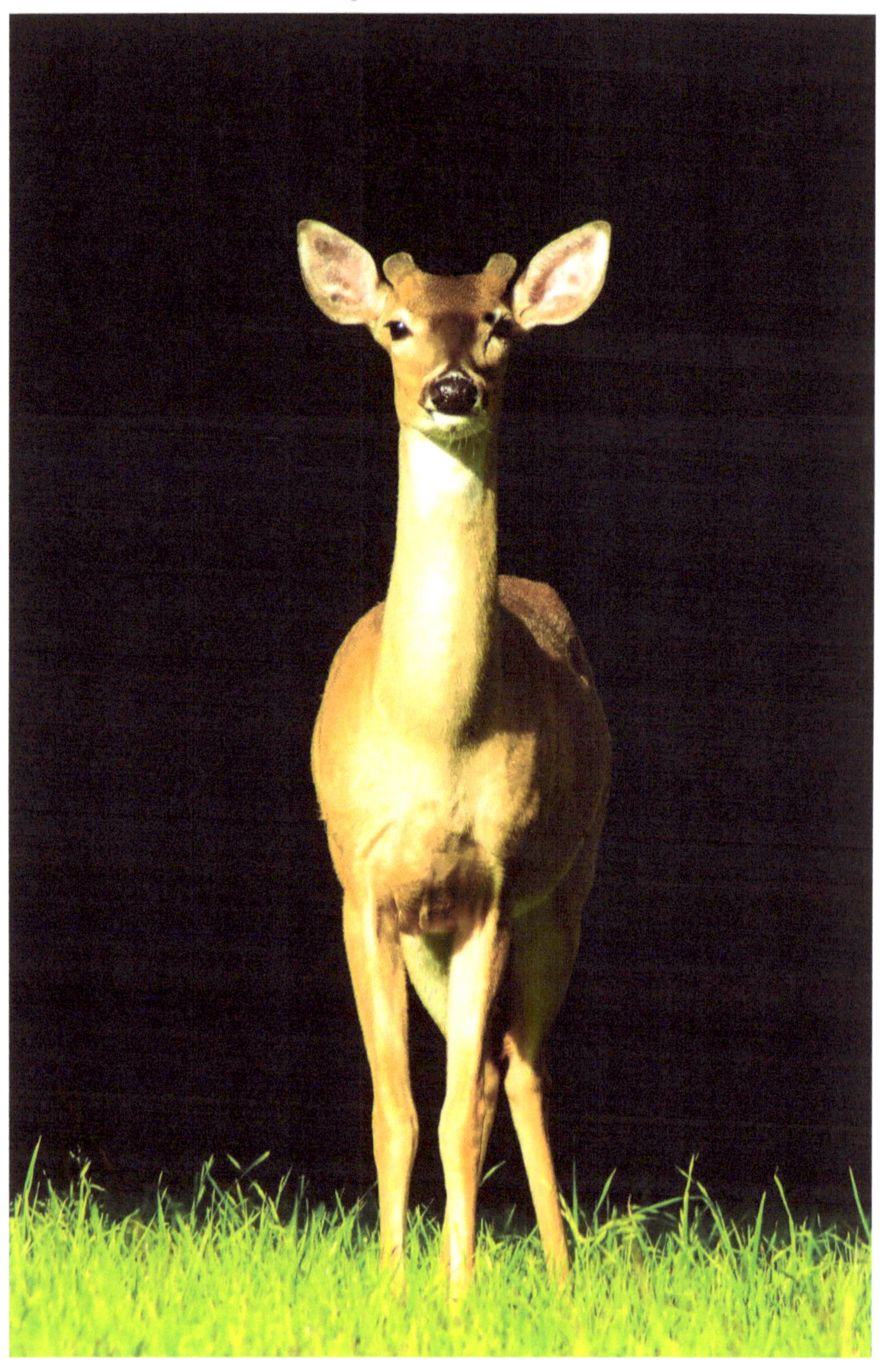

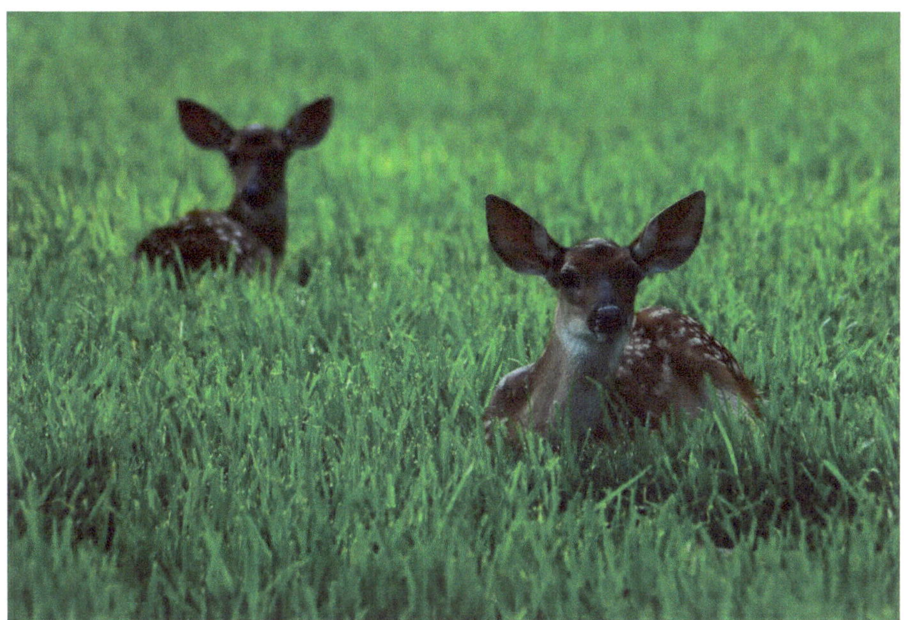

It was the deer that won me over.

A new chapter in our lives. We had accepted it, embraced it even. Starting over in a new city.

But one can never know how things will turn out. It's hard to know what a city is like until you've lived there for three months, six months, more.

Spring break came fast that year. And we were here - in Austin - to find a house. Though we were partially here already. My husband had come in March. My son and I would join him in June when the school year was over.

It was spring, and we were early for the house viewing. All three of us, early morning, looking up at a two-storey house. My husband suggested we drive around the neighborhood, to kill time, to see what the neighborhood was like.

There were trees - oak, cedar. The grass was lush, like an illustration. And then there were the deer.

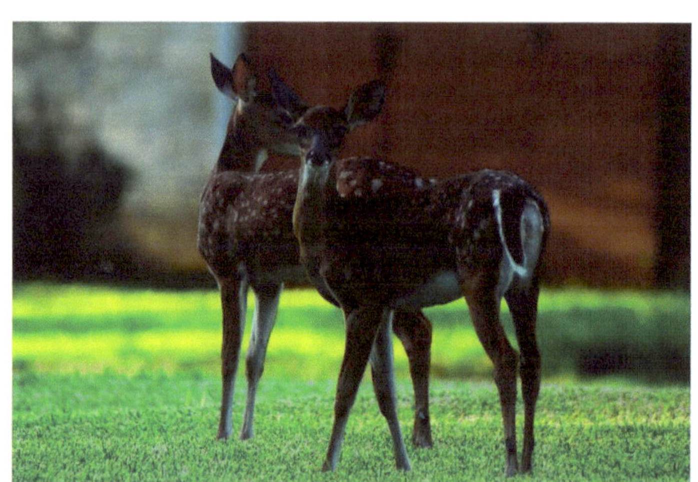

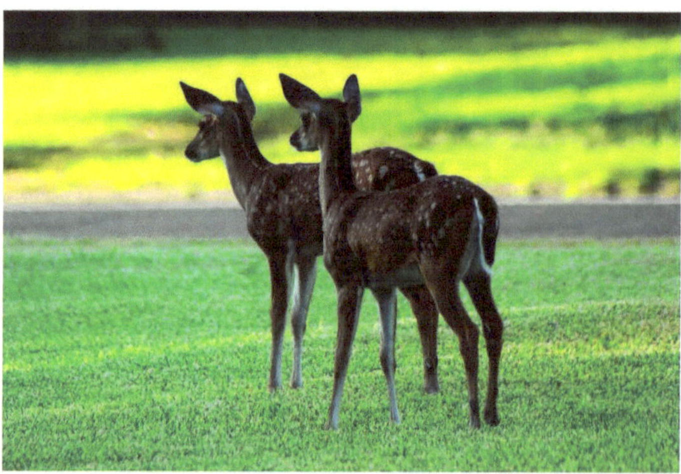

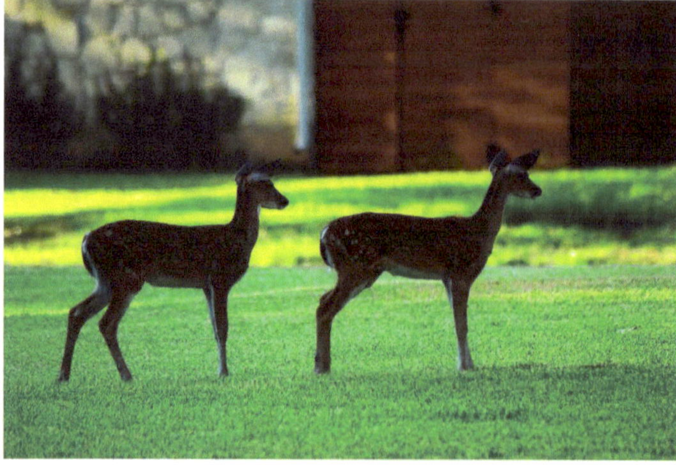

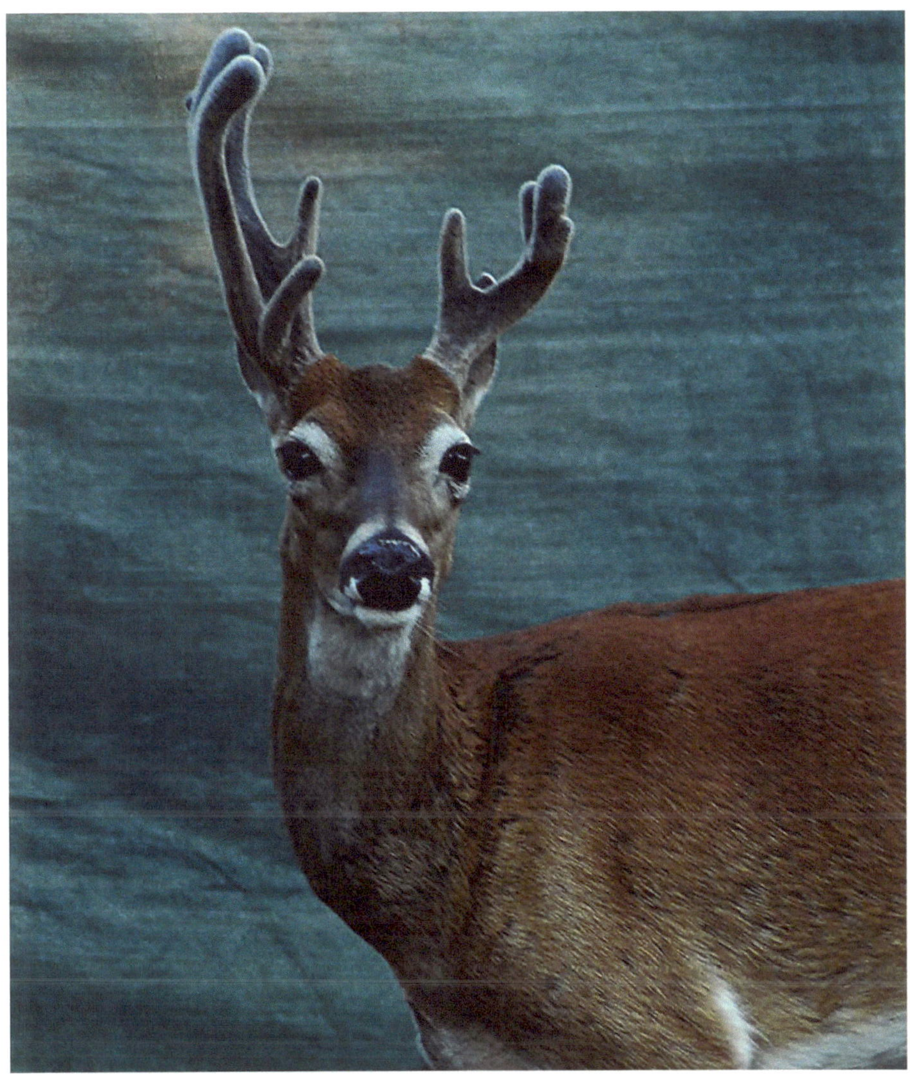

I'm used to them now. But that day, they were a novelty. Angelic even. Big, brown eyes watching us. Wet noses sniffing the air.

Something about that moment has stayed with me. The way we stared at them. The look I exchanged with my son, my husband. The glow in my son's eyes when he has discovered something he loves.

In that moment, I knew. Things would be better here, easier. Life would feel like a gift.

It was the deer that told me. Or, I'd like to believe they did.

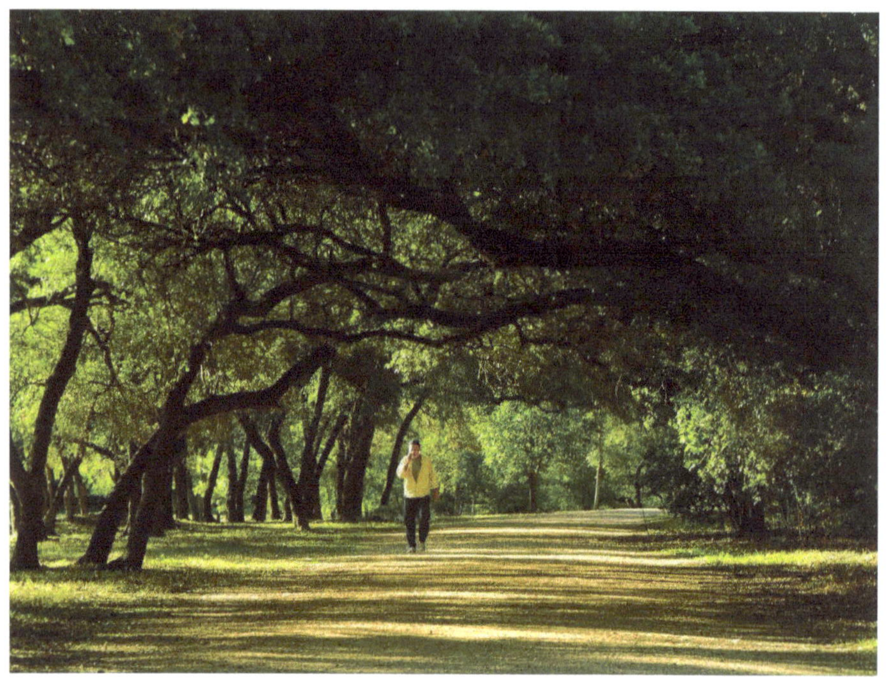

Austin is green in a way other cities aren't. Maybe it has something to do with the oak trees and the way they bend towards our path, stretching their limbs toward us, creating a strange sort of intimacy.

When we first moved to Austin, friends would email me, asking about the "desert" life, and I would surprise them with pictures of lush greenery. The cliche desert landscape from movies or TV shows set in Texas always seems to depict West Texas.

Or maybe that's what people remember.

But Central Texas, the Hill Country, gets quite a bit of rain. And in the spring, the parks and fields explode with colors: Bluebonnets, Pink Evening Primroses, Black-Eyed Susans, Indian Blankets, Winecups, or even the smaller Rain Lilies.

The bluebonnets appear suddenly, almost overnight: blankets of blue stretched out across open fields. And then there are the pink evening primrose flowers. Softer, more delicate. But dominant in their own way.

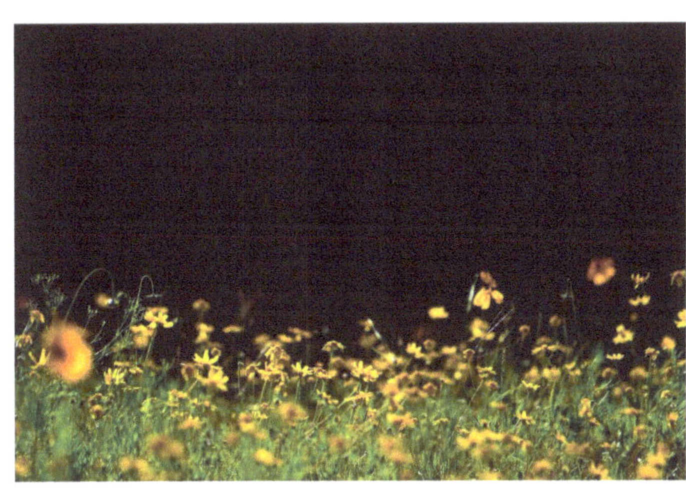

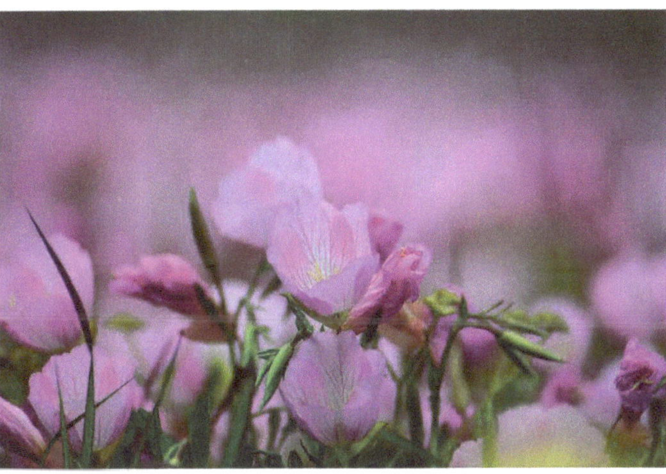

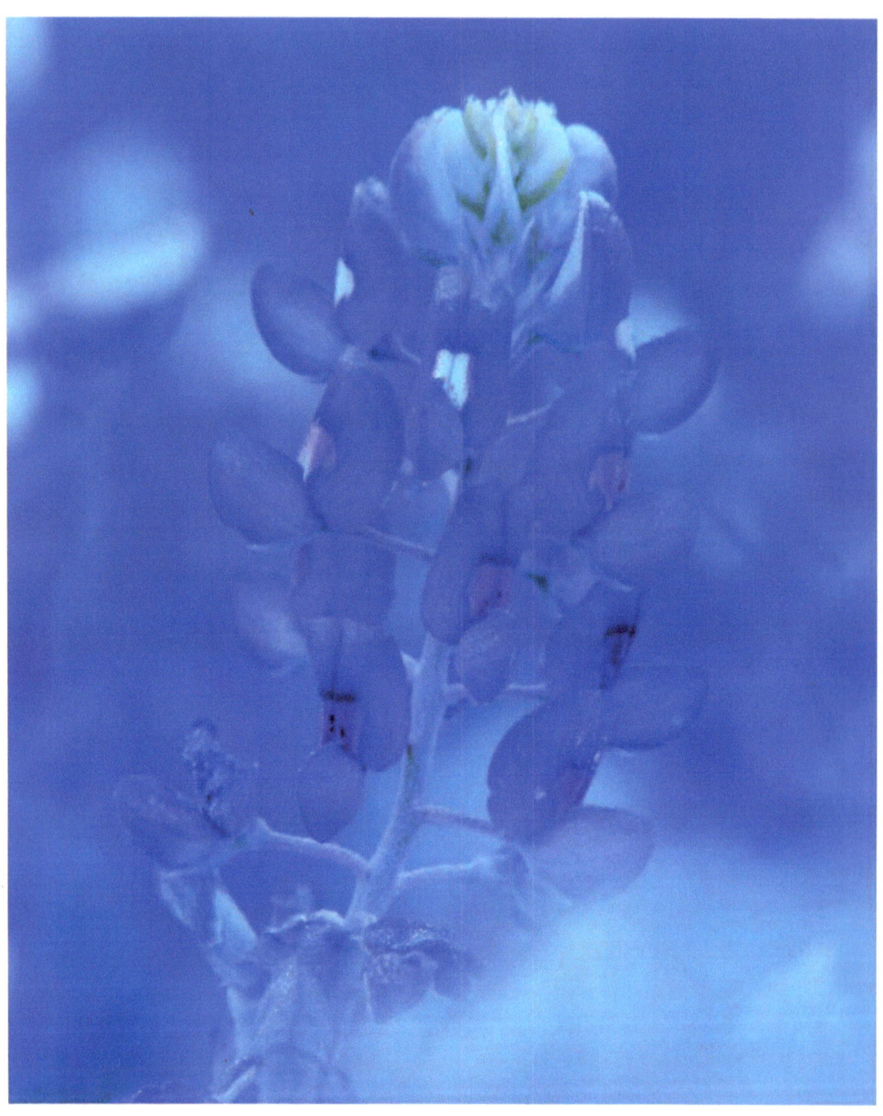

Flowers aren't my favorite subject to photograph, but I read somewhere that you're not a Texas photographer if you don't have a photo of a bluebonnet in your gallery.

Nature is healing. But it can also be scary...

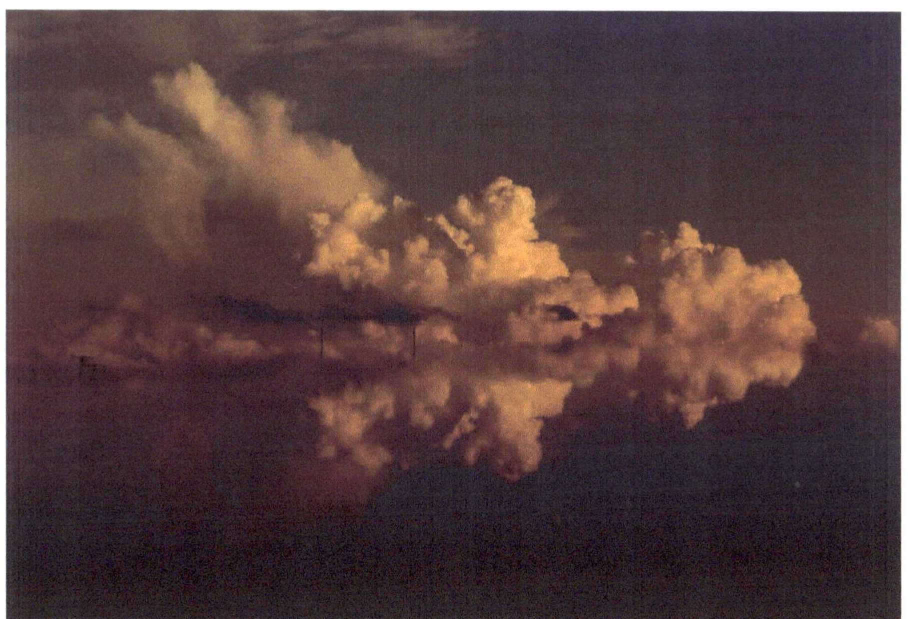

When the thunderstorms are severe and the internet goes out, I write: pen to paper, the way I wrote growing up. The storms threaten the electricity and our appliances, so I run from room to room, unplugging our computers, the TV, our phones, and the air fryer. Anything I wouldn't want to lose in a power surge.

My son's friend lost his Wii game. He was 10 at the time, and it saddened me knowing he returned home from vacation to find his console fried.

Every time I hear a loud crack of thunder, I'm reminded of how powerful nature is and how small we seem when it chooses to dominate. The rain is calming, scary, violent - all at once. And the pop of a siren suddenly suggests how cruel the storm can be. Unfair, even.

We were caught in a severe thunderstorm once. The hail hitting my car felt like it was being struck by small pebbles. We finally took cover under a tarp on the side of the road, waiting for the storm to abate.

An hour and a half later, the sun was out, and there was little indication of the chaos before. Only the clouds suggested something was amiss, like someone had painted a message in the sky saying, A storm was here.

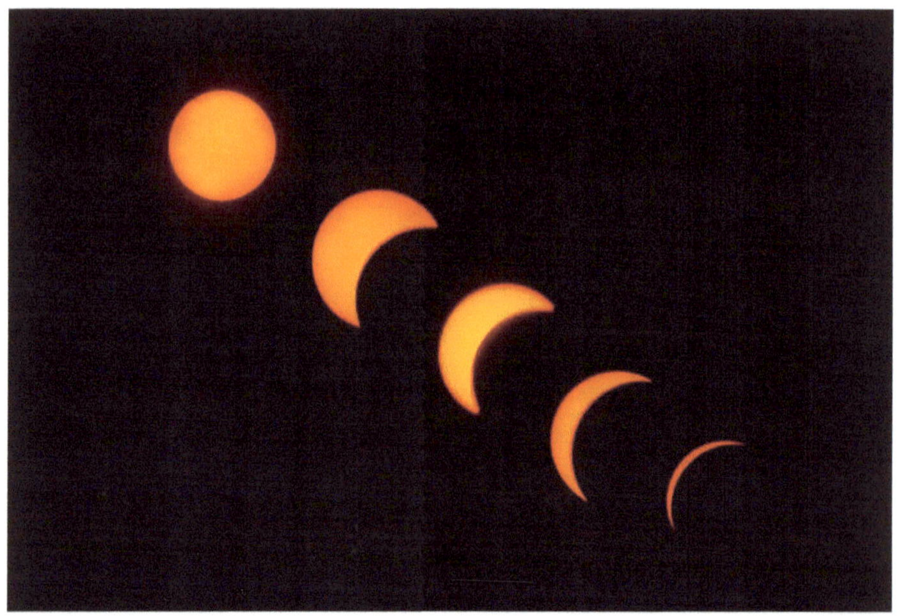

So this is how spring comes every year. Storms, rain, sun, and puddles. Indecisively tip-toeing in, unsure. Almost asking winter for permission.

Spring of 2024: Texans are "lucky." We're on the path of the 2024 total solar eclipse. But the weather forecast predicts it's going to be an overcast and rainy day. I'm disappointed, to say the least.

In 2017, a total eclipse passed through Oregon. That year, I took my 8-year-old son out of school and we flew to the southern coast of the state. My mother and her husband joined us from New York, and our eclipse trip turned out to be one of the best "vacations" we've had.

This year, we'll be watching it from our backyard.

On eclipse day, April 8th, I wake up to an overcast sky. I'm not expecting the skies to clear, but I'm still hopeful. I get my camera, lens, and sun filter ready. I also lay out our eclipse glasses. Every thirty minutes, I check the sky. At 12:10, I notice the sun peeking through every so often.

After lunch, I lay blankets out on our garden deck and wait. The sun juts in and out from behind the clouds as the moon begins its journey. For some reason, this makes me excited, knowing I only have a few seconds to steal a shot before the sun slithers away again.

At full totality, our backyard darkens and the streetlight turns on. Four minutes of darkness. We sit in an almost awestruck silence.

I look up at the sky. It's overcast, and it remains that way for the four minutes of totality.

I don't mind.

I won't get to capture totality with my camera, but being plunged into darkness at 1:36 p.m. seems far more fascinating.

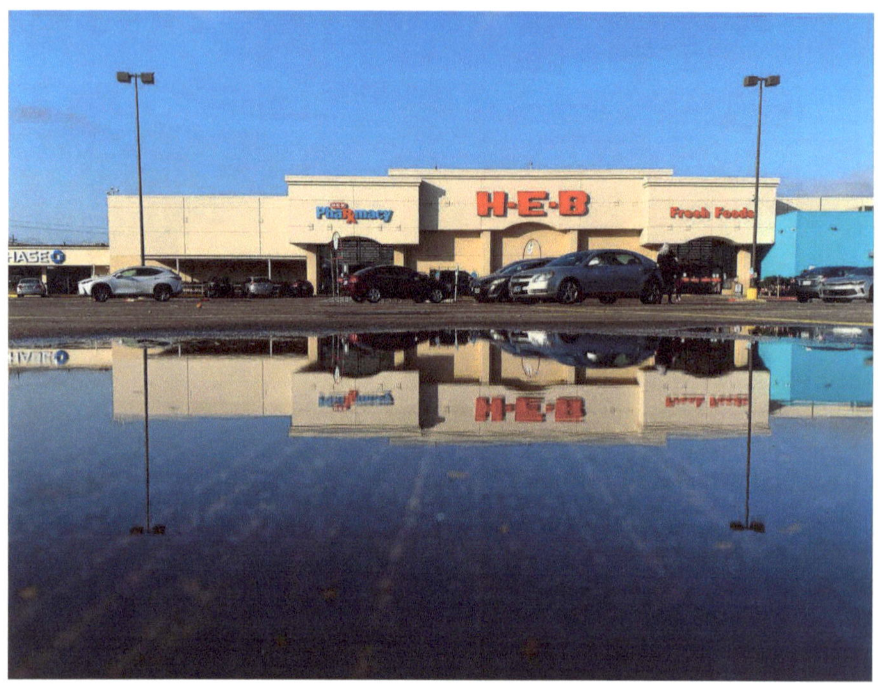

The H-E-B grocery store is king

Chasing Puddles...

When it rains, I chase puddles, and I chase them like they're a news story, rushing to the scene before they disappear, praying that they're large enough or that the drive over is worth it.

The rain has become an ally, a welcome partner every spring, whether it's sheets of rain or sprinkles throughout the day. Rain in the forecast means I get a break from watering the garden, and a little magic for my photography.

I look for potholes where the rain can collect or dips in the cement when the streets collide with the sidewalks. I curse when a property is too level, too... perfect. In the end, I have no control over the puddles that will show up, so I simply take what I can get.

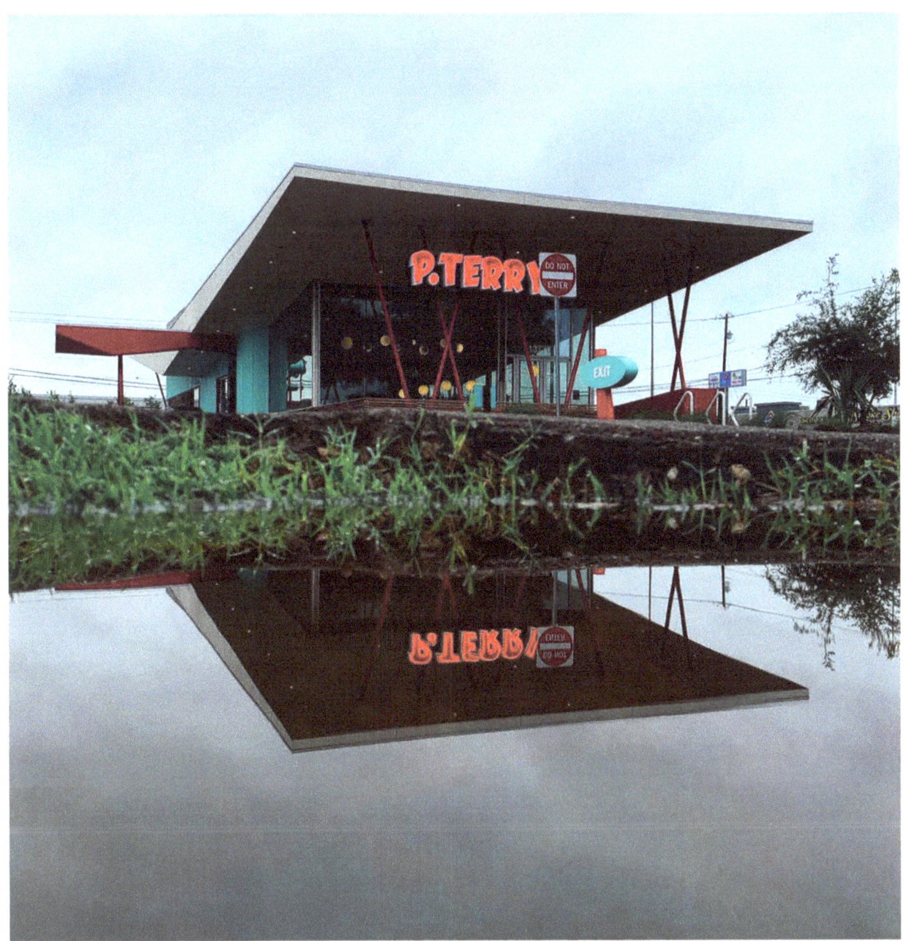

Austin's P. Terry's - architect Michael Hsu

The puddles force me to notice Austin's buildings, architecture, and landmarks. Which means I have my favorites. So, if I have to choose between Texas's Whataburger or Austin's P. Terry's, I'd choose Whataburger (their Patty Melt).

But let me go back.

The P. Terry's structure stands out, a spaceship design, futuristic architecture that catches your eye. I'm eager to try all things Austin, eat a burger in one of Austin's own.

Friday. After school. We make an informal date to try out Austin's fast food joint. I order my usual, a cheeseburger, and wait, watching the afternoon light streak through the futuristic interiors.

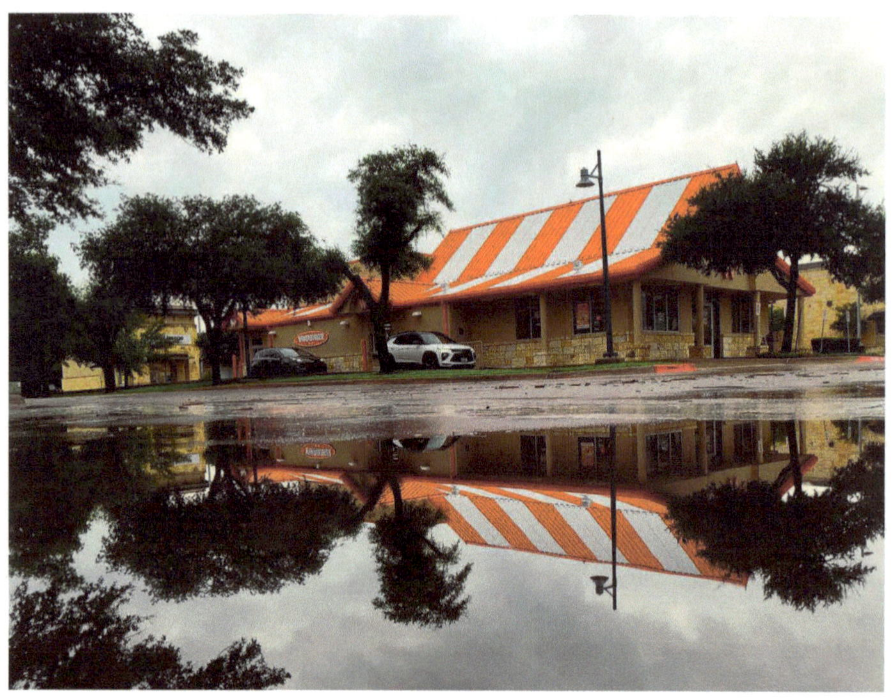

Texas's Whataburger

The food comes, and I stare at it, disappointed. The cheese is cold, unmelted. Is this normal for P. Terry's? I don't ask, simply assume it is. Cold cheese on a warm burger isn't appealing. We don't go back.

But one day, driving down Barton Springs Rd, I see an ad: P. Terry's, a cheeseburger, melted cheese. And then I think: was there a mistake? Online, I do research. There are two negative reviews ... unmelted cheese. One has photos. It was a mistake then. Maybe bad service. I vow never to return.

Recently, though, my son's school has a fundraiser there. I'm obligated now.

So, we return. This time, I try the banana bread and the oatmeal chocolate chip cookie. Again, we sit in the futuristic interiors.

The gray, bland sky that afternoon reflects how I feel: disappointed. My son wants me to like the food, seems bruised that I don't. So, I say, maybe to appease him, "At least I like the architecture."

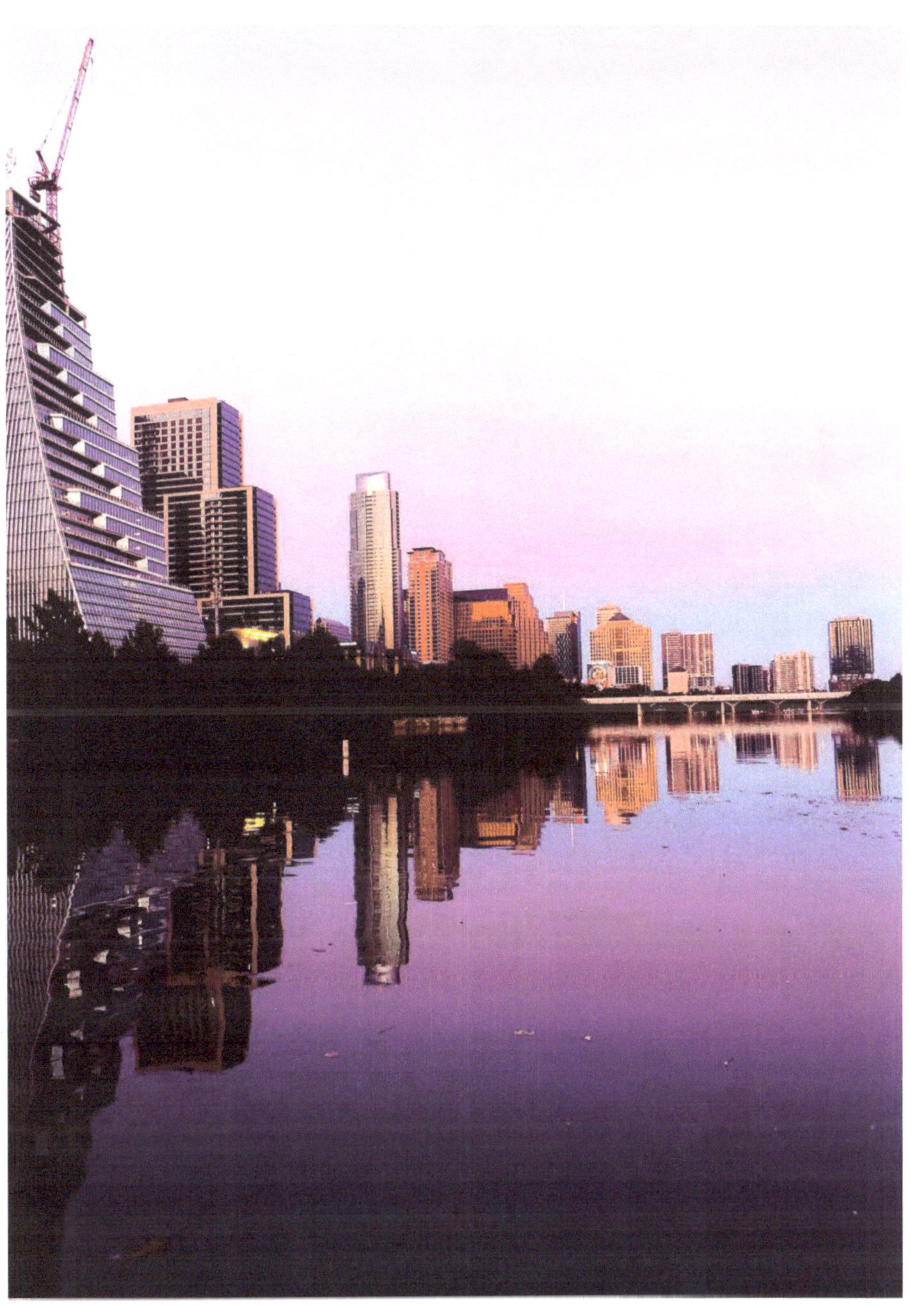

Downtown Austin, Sep 2021

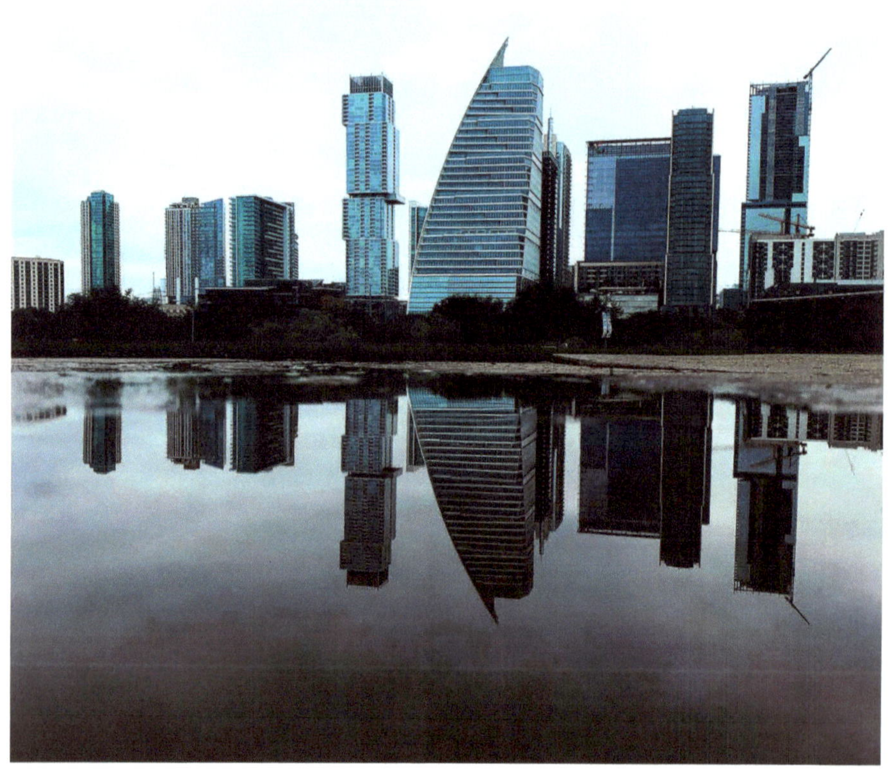

I watch Austin's evolving architecture through my Lady Bird Lake photo reflections.

Block 185, Austin's "Google Tower," was incomplete in September of 2019, but topped out two years later. More and more skyscrapers dot Austin's skyline.

Whereas many older Austinites find the new changes disconcerting, I find the bluish and glassy skyline beautiful. The changes seem endless, I'll admit, and every time I take a new city reflection photo of downtown Austin from the hike-and-bike trail, I notice cranes that weren't previously there.

I'm a little in awe at how fast a city can expand. The 183 S. freeway has added another lane in an attempt to ease traffic congestion, and apartment complexes are sprouting up like rabbits.

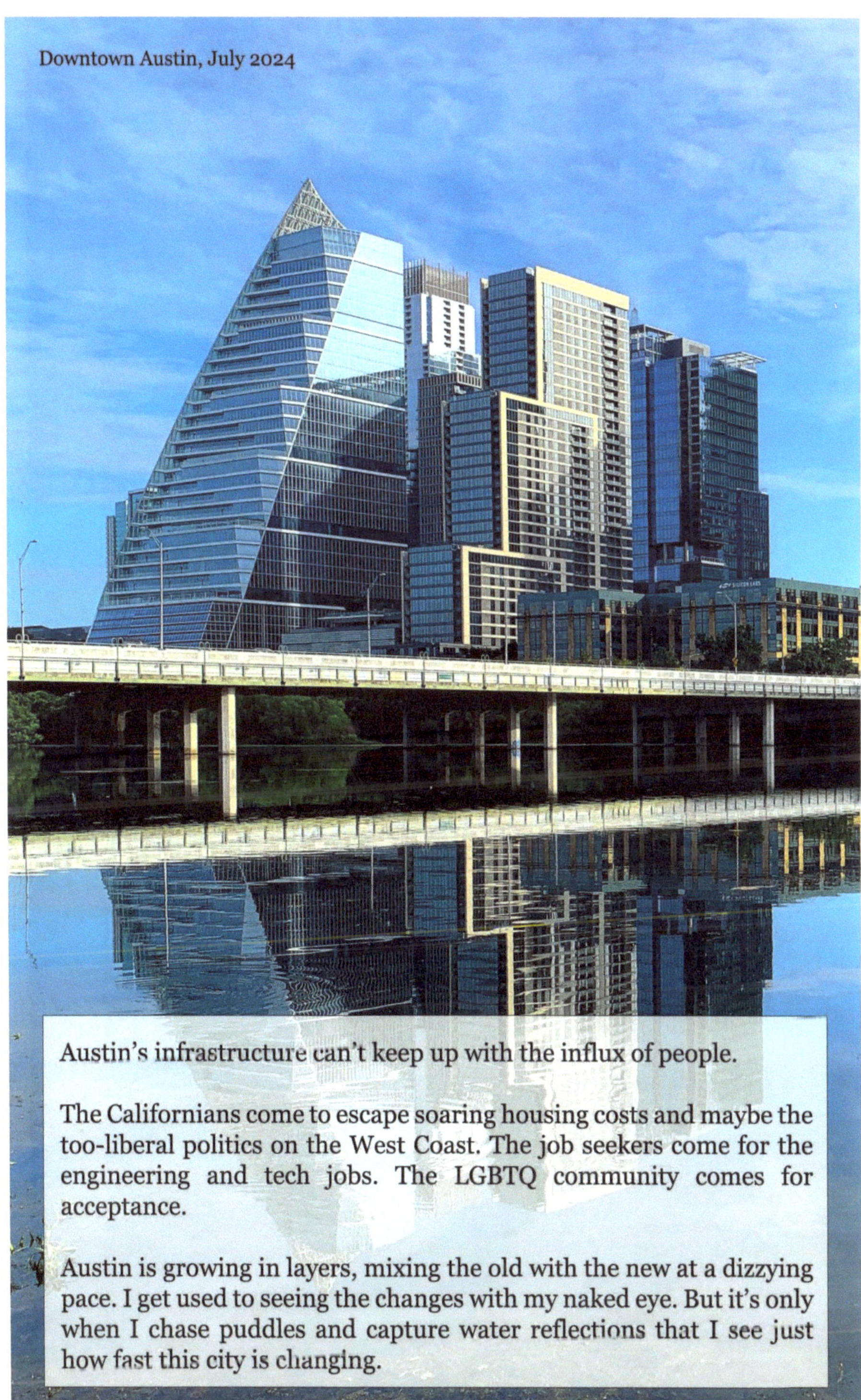

Austin's infrastructure can't keep up with the influx of people.

The Californians come to escape soaring housing costs and maybe the too-liberal politics on the West Coast. The job seekers come for the engineering and tech jobs. The LGBTQ community comes for acceptance.

Austin is growing in layers, mixing the old with the new at a dizzying pace. I get used to seeing the changes with my naked eye. But it's only when I chase puddles and capture water reflections that I see just how fast this city is changing.

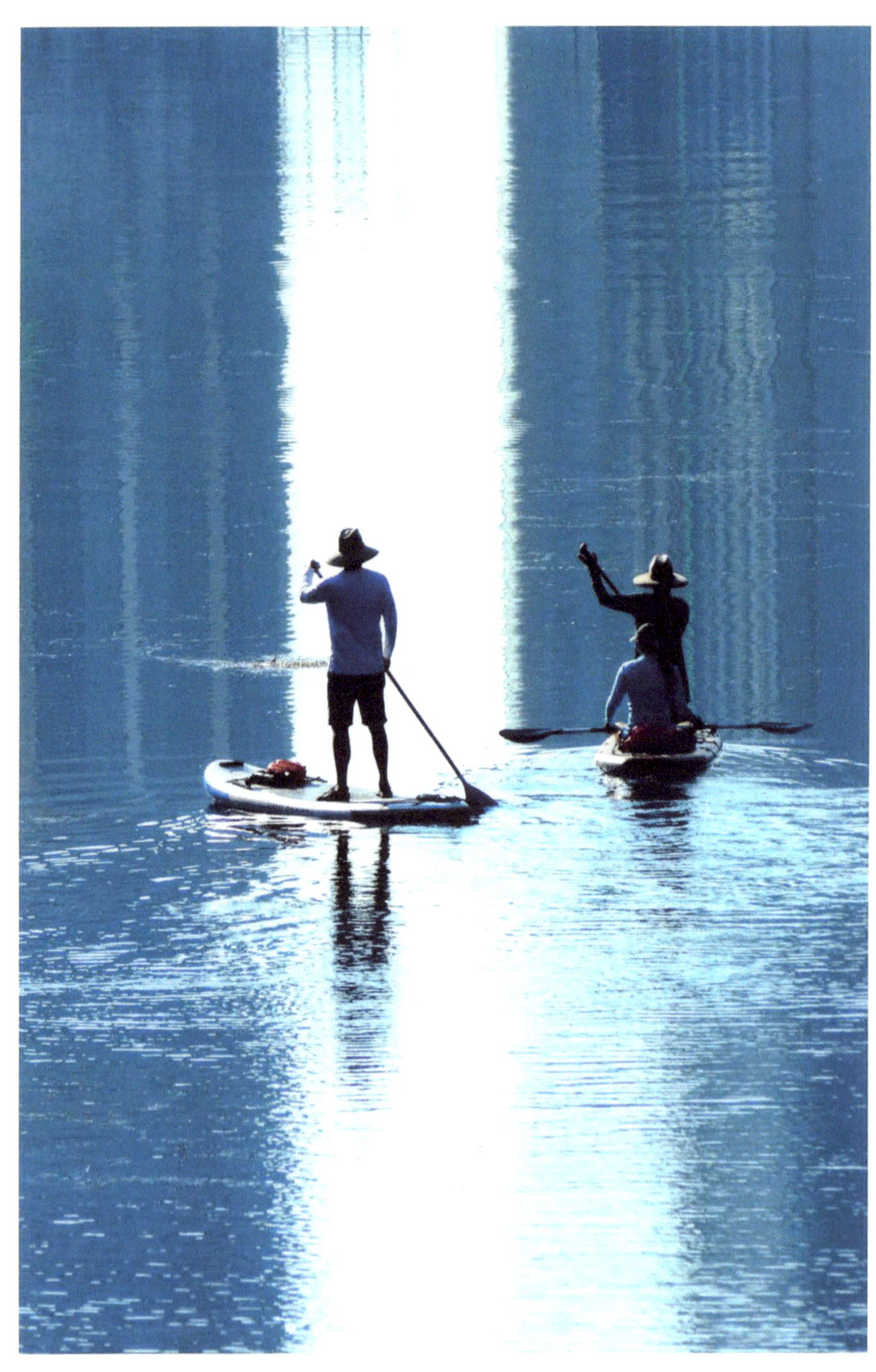

Kayaking on Lady Bird Lake, downtown Austin

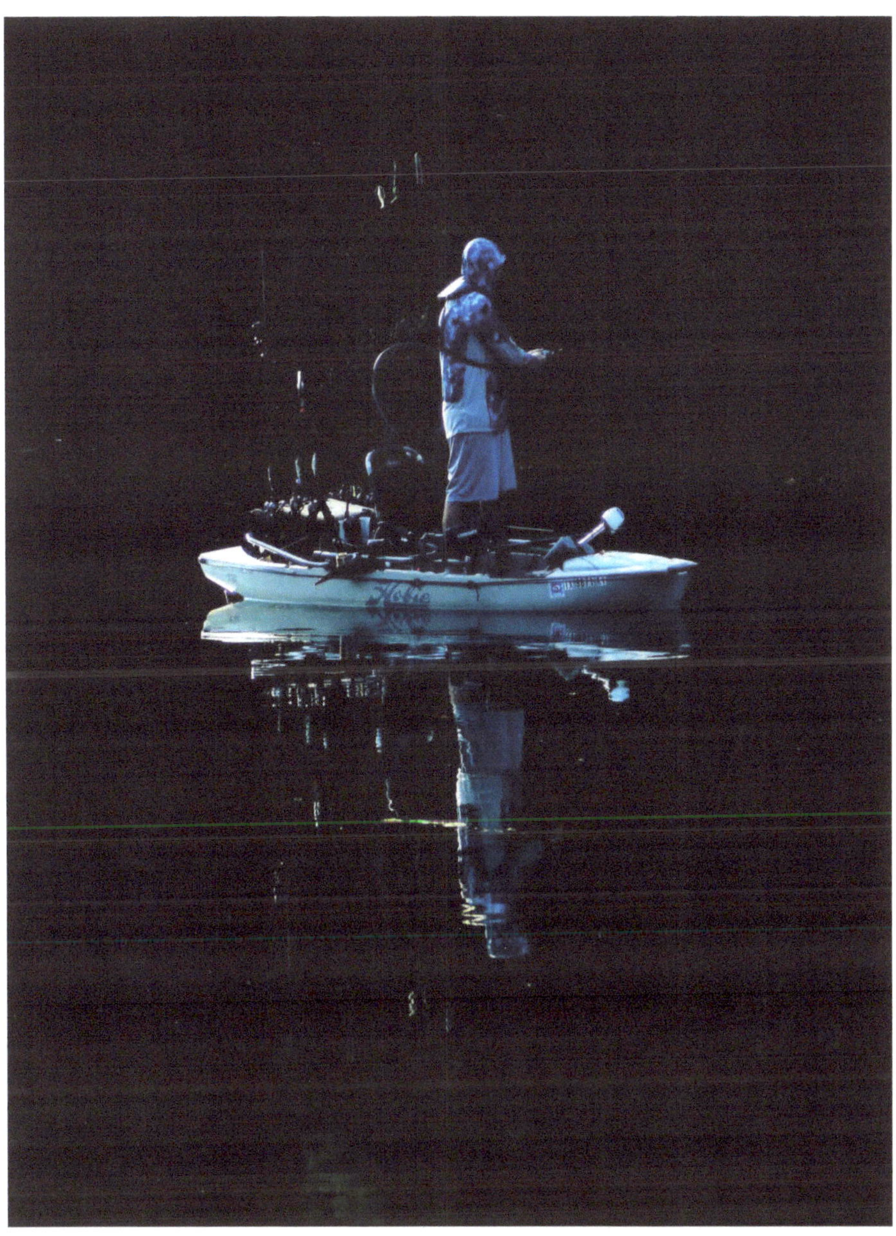

Fishing in Lady Bird Lake, downtown Austin

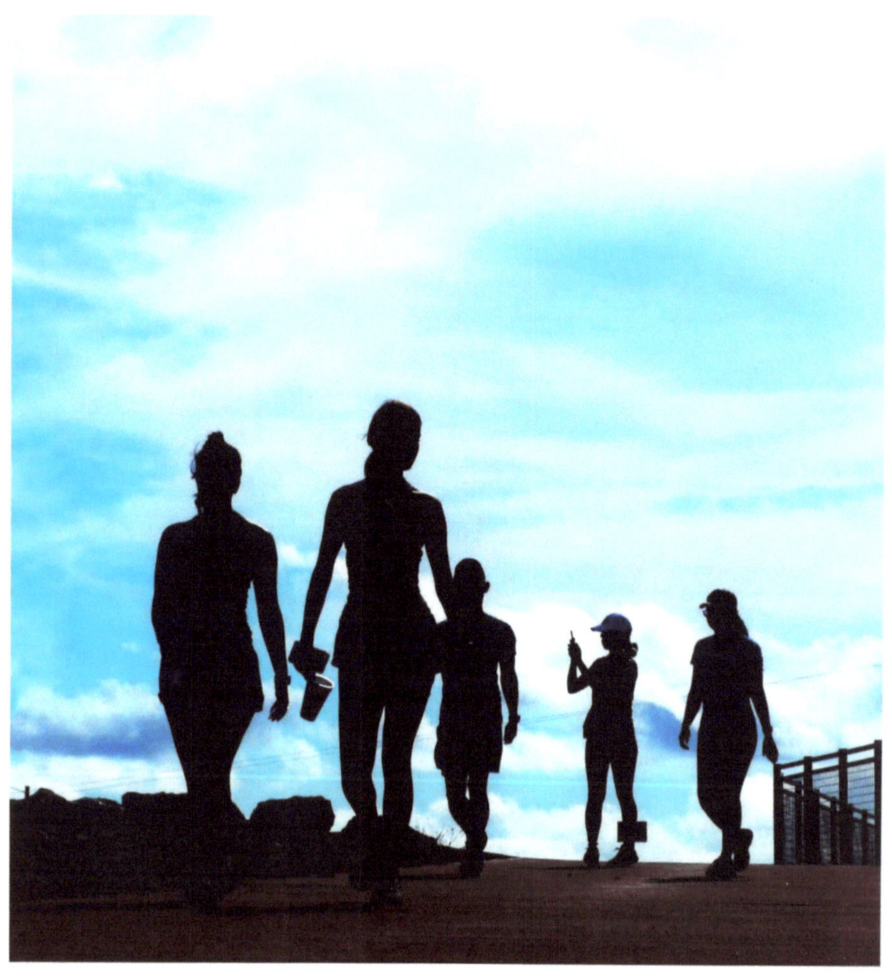

Someone told me it takes 6 months to discover a city. But it took me 2 years to discover Brushy Creek Park. There's a lake, a bridge, trees, flowers. I rarely take photos of any of that, though. I like the silhouettes. Black, moving figures against a pure blue sky or a moody one.

I come here for the nature, but my camera seems transfixed by the people — both new and old. They emerge in the spring, like flowers, crowding the trails. In pairs, in groups, alone.

A city is defined by its people.

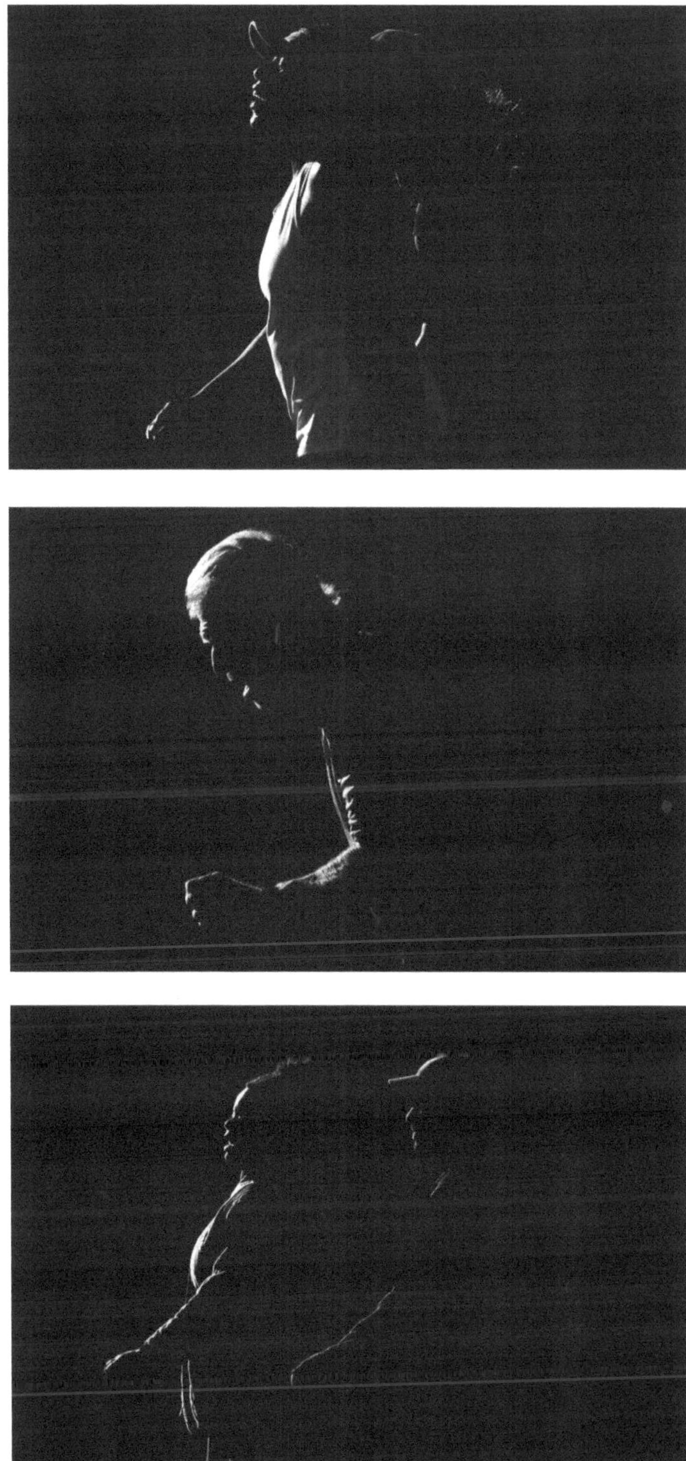

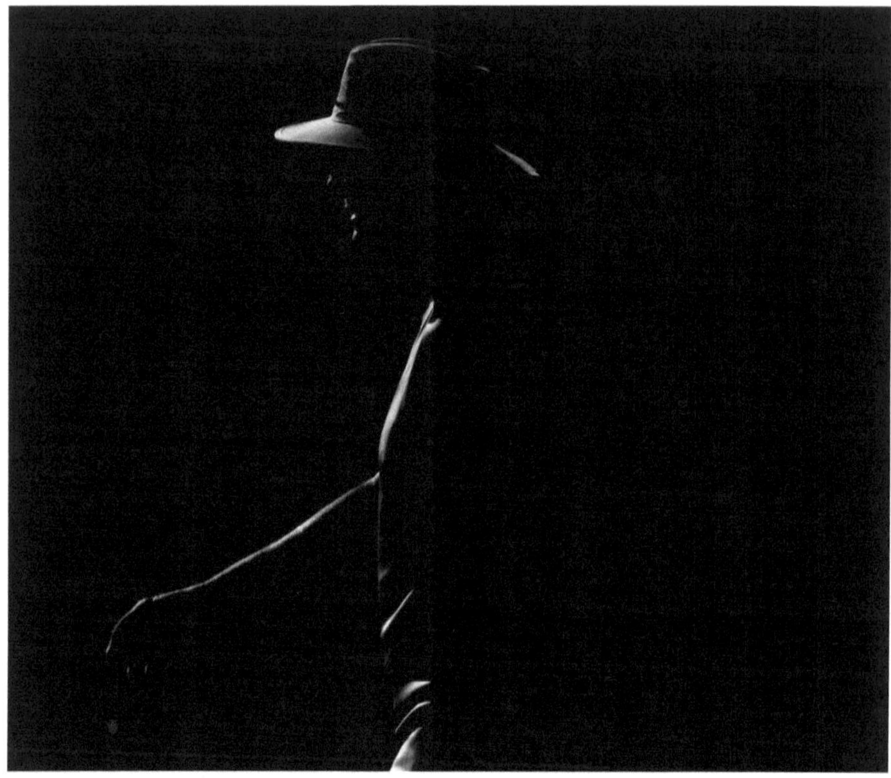

Sometimes, I sit in the middle section of a trail, people watching. Lifting my camera every time the rim lighting catches someone just right. It's the absence of light on their bodies or just enough light on their edges that fascinates me.

I feel at peace in this park. Or as a friend said when I showed her a photo of pure green on my trails: Shinrin-Yoku. Forest-bathing in Japanese. Connecting and meditating in nature.

Every Sunday, it's what I do here. Meditate on my morning run.

The park is beautiful, and I tell myself that one day, soon, I'll photograph the nature here. Or kayak on the lake. Or have a picnic on a bench, facing the water.

But for now, people watching is enough.

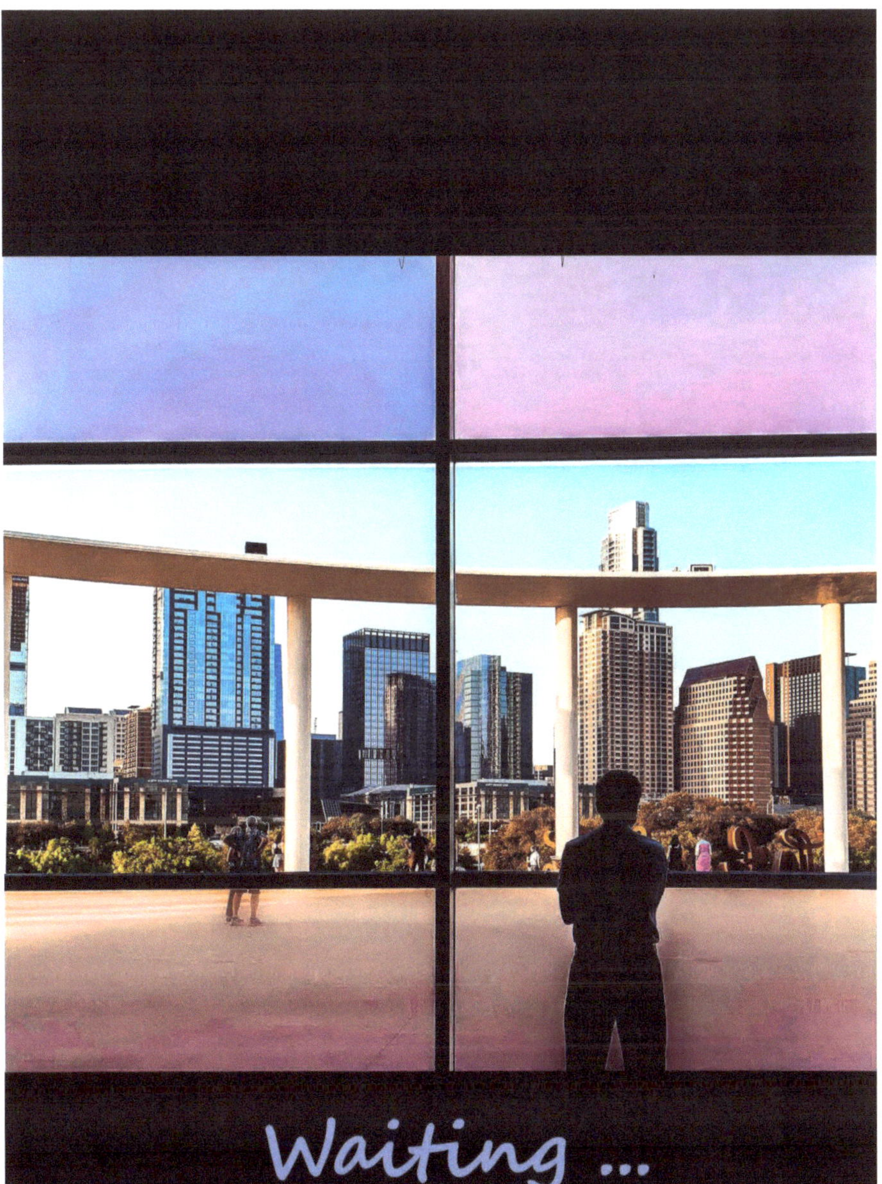
Waiting ...

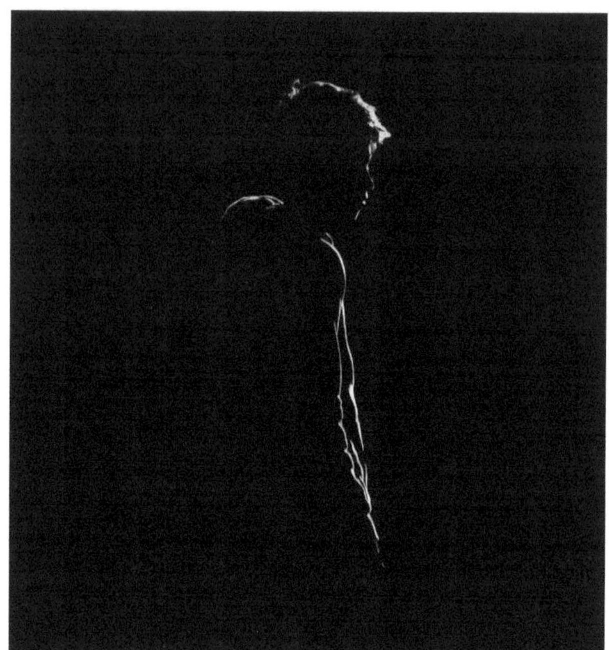

Waiting for the schoool bus

I do a lot of waiting in Austin. Waiting for a show to start at the Long Center, waiting to pick my son up from school, waiting for his rock climbing class to end.

I also wait more than I should because I arrive early to appointments, shows, or meetings, afraid that I'll get caught in traffic or get lost. My son doesn't like how I plan things: allowing time for traffic or giving myself extra time in case I take the wrong exit. And it irritates him when we're too early (a good thing I think, because I didn't get lost). This means he has about 20 minutes to stare out at the horizon, bored. It also means he loses 20 minutes of his time at home, playing video games.

It's nice to be bored, sometimes, I tell him. Healthy even. It gives you time to think, be creative. He reflects on this and then comes up with other video games he may want to play, to purchase. When he says this, I think how limited the minds of 10-year-old boys must be.

But I'm being unfair.

I have my journals going all the way back to when I was twelve. I'm embarrassed to re-read what I wrote, mainly because it's peppered with what I wore and other inconsequential, shallow meanderings. So I don't judge.

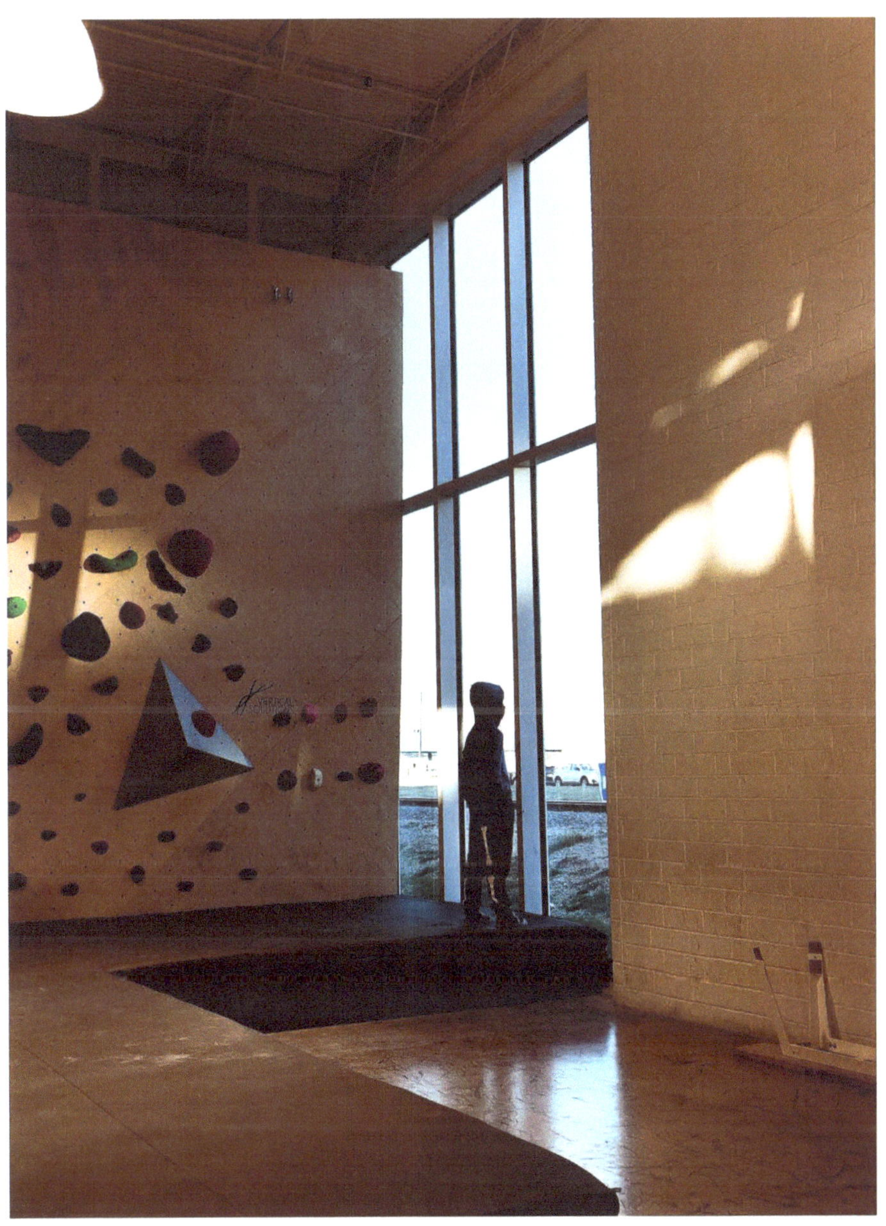

Waiting for rock climbing class to start

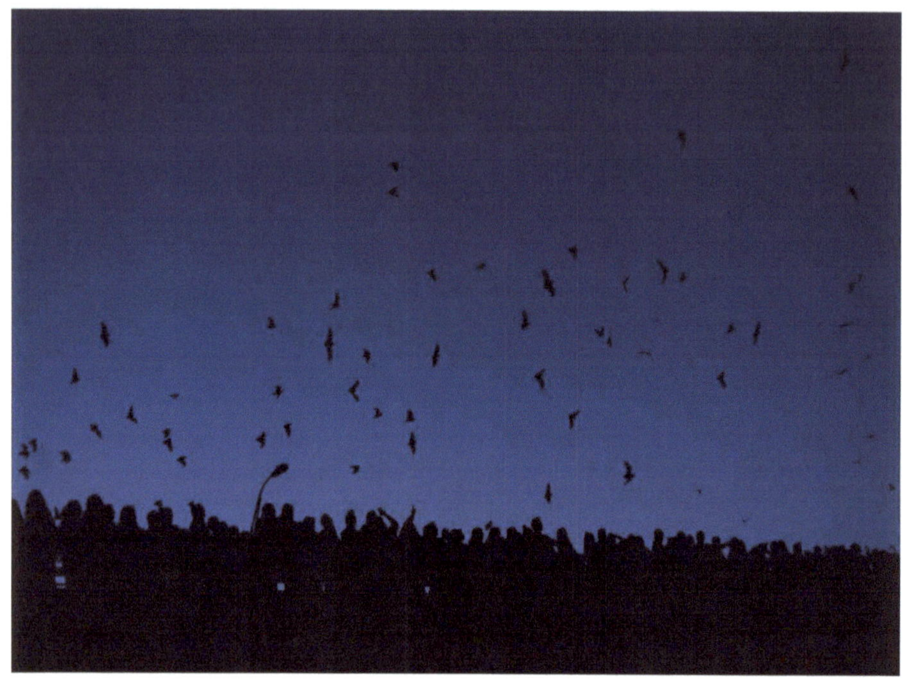

Still, I do a lot of waiting. I wait for the bats. I wait for the sky to darken. I wait for the crowds to thicken, watching as the line extends along Congress Bridge. I've been coming to watch the bats for five years now. The first time as a tourist. The other times as a resident.

Sometimes, I end up talking with those sitting around me. Other times, I stare at the growing crowd, silently.

When the bats emerge, there's a round of applause, like the bats are actors making their Broadway entrance. Do they know we're applauding them with bated breath every night from March until early September? Or are they bothered by our gawking presence as we stand in the way of their nightly hunt?

Like the curtain preparing to open, the sky changes colors. The bats are backstage now, starting to stir from their sleep, watching the growing audience in their seats from behind the curtains. Or, maybe they're listening to our chatter, irritated. These are female bats, and we must be bothering their babies. I get the feeling they're emerging later and later every year, hoping we'll slowly disappear.

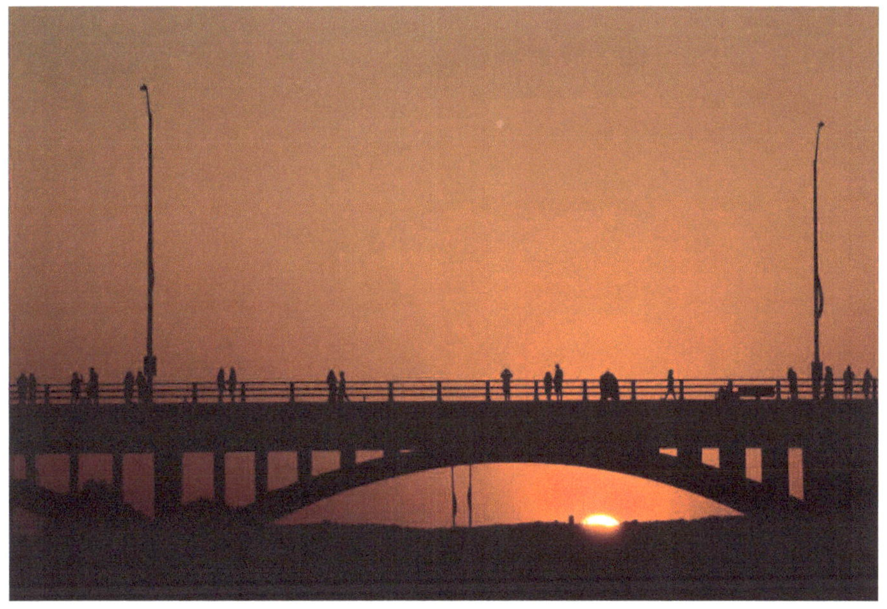

I haven't seen the bats emerge since 2020, though I catch lots of sunsets.

9:22 p.m. The sky is dark. I wait. The crowd waits. Today, I chat with a couple from Houston. This is their first time seeing the bats, and I wish I could tell them that this isn't usual, that the bats have already made their entrance by this time.

Last time it was 8:40 p.m. I'm sure. Though last time wasn't humid.

My DSLR camera doesn't pick up anything anymore. The sky looks black, and the street lights are on.

We wait a little longer. But, today, the bats don't come.

An Interruption
for Covid

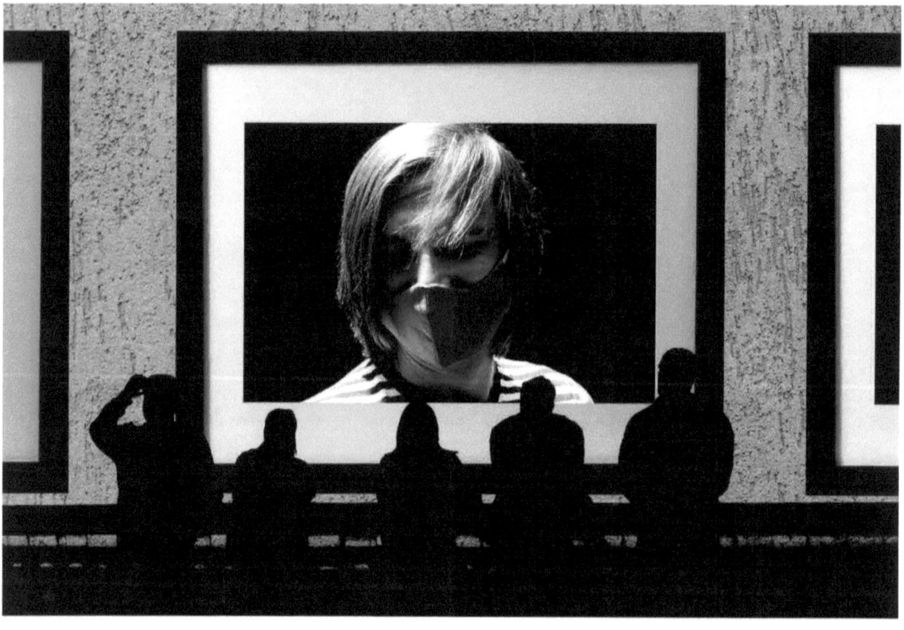

The pandemic becomes real for me on March 17th when my husband calls to say his company has shut down and everything is closed until further notice.

I work from home and my income is not affected. In fact, in retrospect, I'm one of the lucky ones.

But the thinning crowds in restaurants and the eerily empty malls feel like a door slowly closing to your room, locking you in.

Everything seems okay, until it isn't.

Austin issues a shelter-at-home order a week later, on March 24th. And a mask mandate is issued on April 14th.

I'm overly optimistic about the pandemic, thinking it will be over in 2 months. My husband says 6 months. My son, a happy equilibrium between the two of us, says 4 months.

We're all wrong.

6 months later, on Sep 15th, in-school learning starts in Austin. It's optional, and I'm on the fence about my decision. But my son begs to go to school — the only time I will ever hear him beg to sit in a classroom.

I agree.

When school starts, only 30% of parents agree to in-school learning. Two-thirds remain virtual.

The school parking lot is relatively empty, which means I can park on school grounds, at the bottom of the slightly sloping school's driveway, and wait to pick my son up.

When people ask where Austin stands regarding schools, these are the photos I send. Our kids are in school. Mandatory masks.

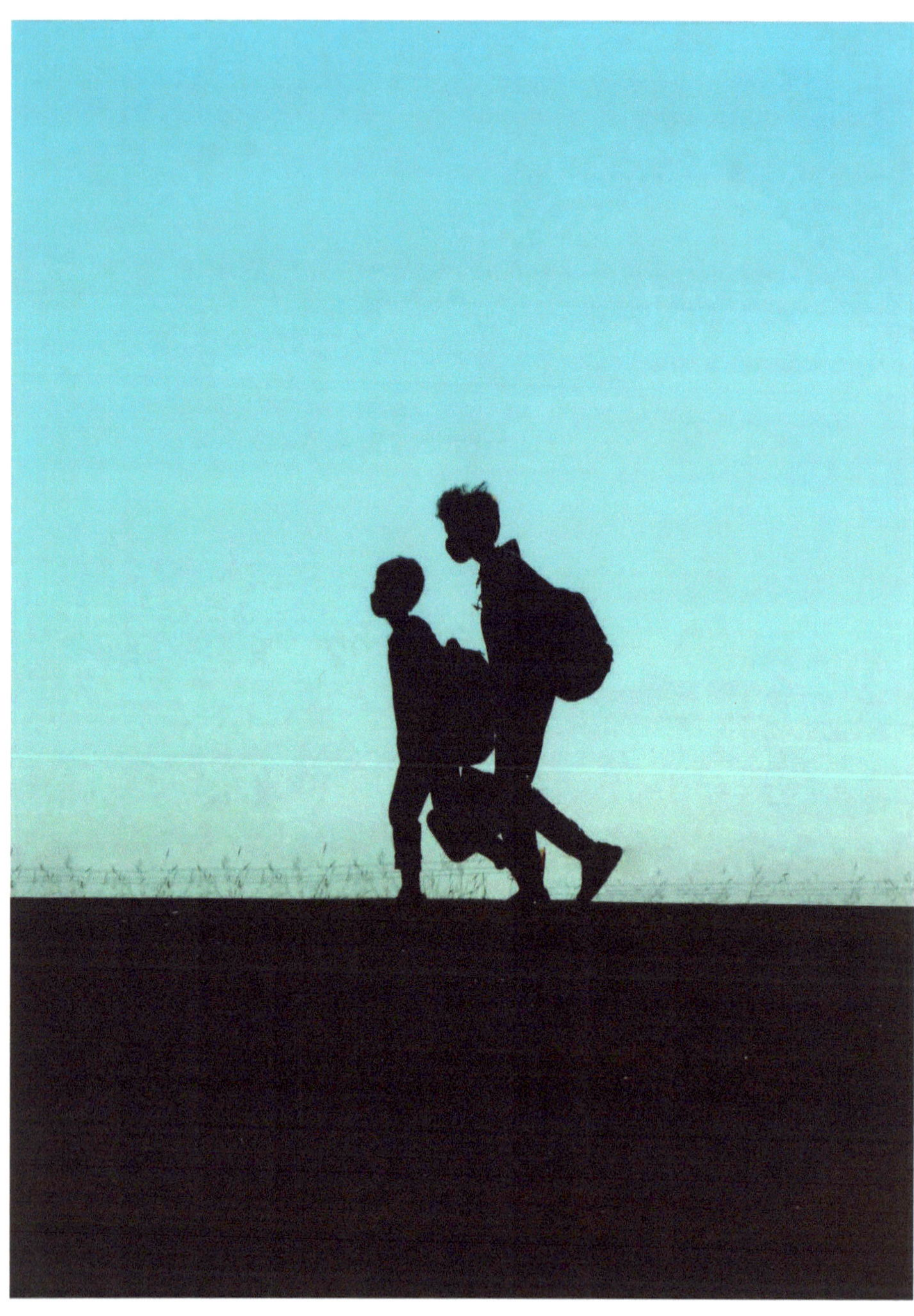

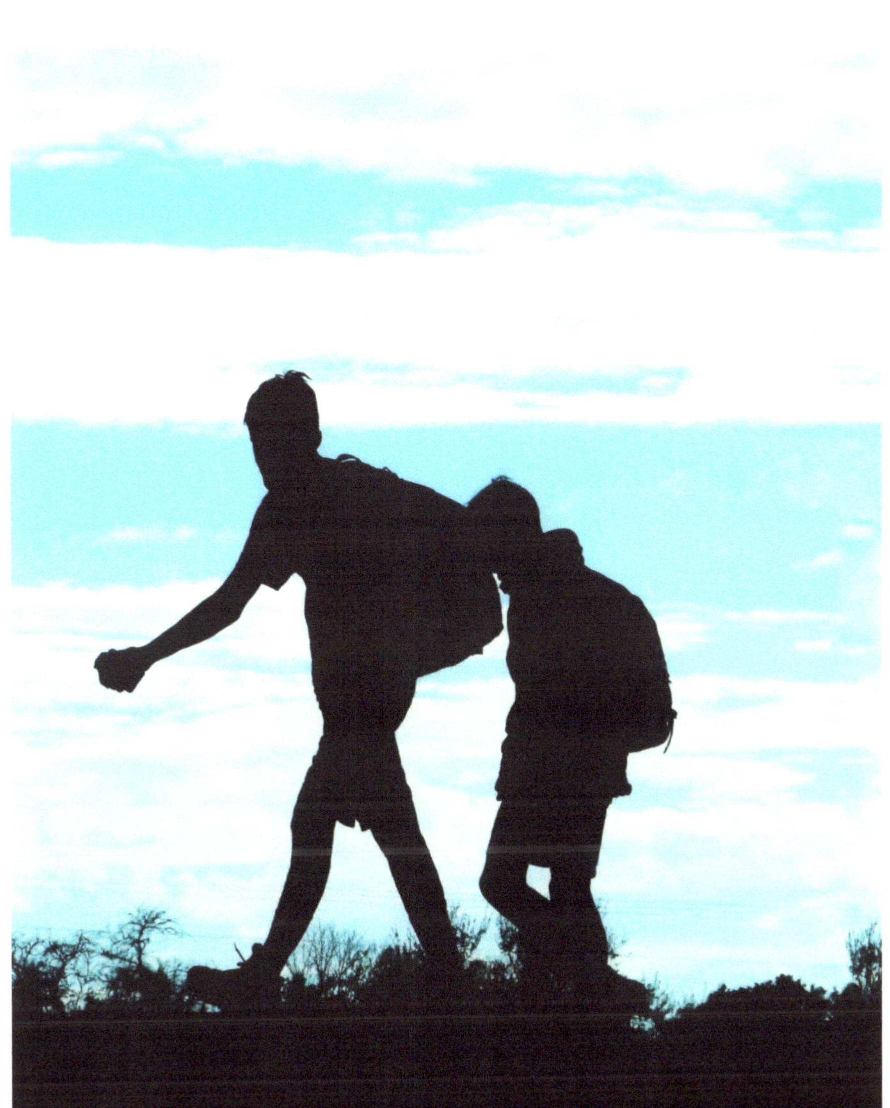

Every 6 weeks, parents receive a new questionnaire. By the 2nd semester, 50% of kids are back in school. And after the 1st semester, I stop worrying. I know my son will be fine.

In the end, we all catch Covid, a year or so later. My husband's symptoms are the worst. Mine are mild, a day of aches. My son feels nothing.

I look back on these days, and I have learned not to judge. Everyone did what they felt was best for themselves and their families. Some chose safety. Some freedom. Some chose to prioritize their mental health.

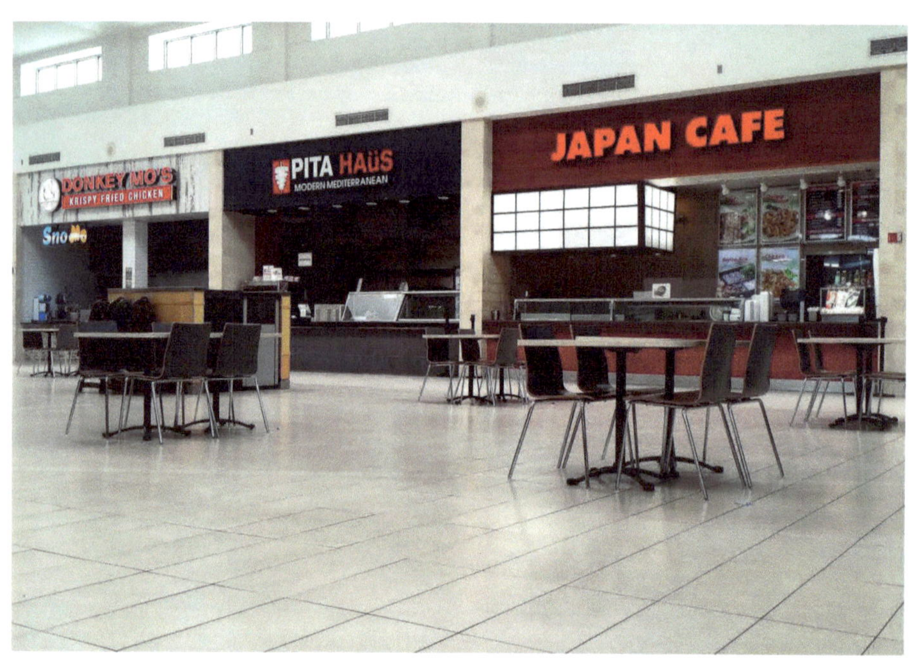

An empty Lakeline mall on May 15th, 2020

Austin reopens at 25% capacity on May 1st, 2020, but the streets are empty and things feel surreal, confined, and apocalyptic.

I ache to see humans again, to be in the midst of crowds. But even on my morning runs or while walking my dog, strangers cross the street to avoid sharing the sidewalk.

We take a road trip to small-town Texas where the people are defiant. There are no masks in sight.

I'm not sure whether to feel comforted by the maskless faces or worried. But life feels normal here, and the apocalypse distant.

The underground church at our hotel fascinates me. Church services on vacation — only in the Bible Belt.

Our road trip is the first time I get a real look behind the curtain and see "true Texas." Religion. Gun stores. Chicken fried steak. The extra large pickup trucks. A desire for little to no government interference. And very friendly people.

Texans are some of the friendliest people I've met.

Four years later, when life feels normal again and the memories of the lockdown blur at the edges, I think of how the state's character surfaced and dictated just how much Texans chose to deal with the pandemic.

In retrospect, it was the pandemic that made me truly understand Texan pride.

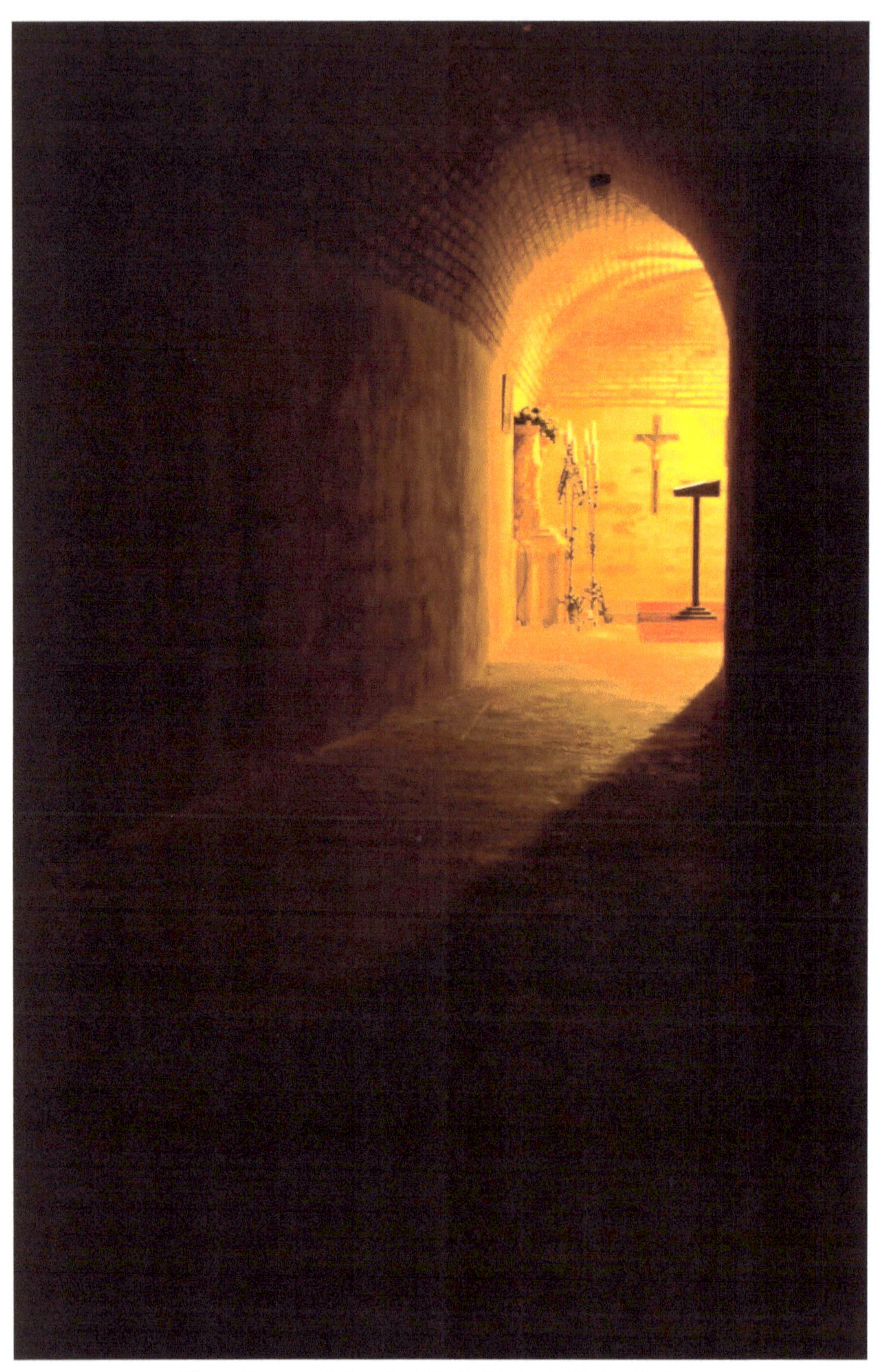

The underground church at Trois Estates in Fredericksburg

Summer

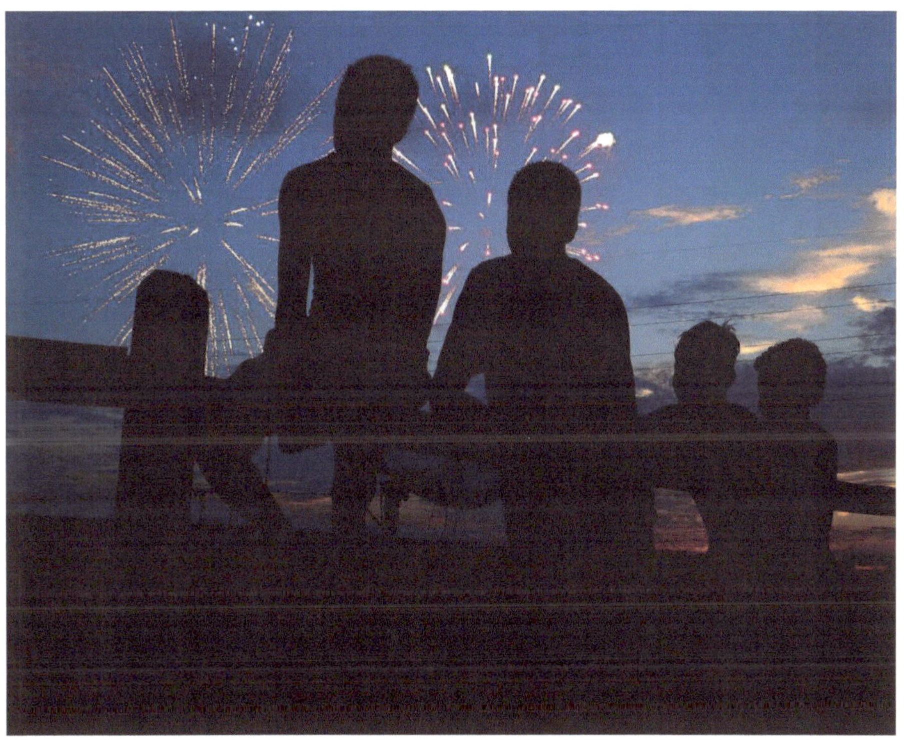

Summer hits hard. Always. A blanket of heat that's oppressive, like an oven that someone switched on.

We moved to Austin in early June. Late spring. But the weather said otherwise.

The sun baked my head, and I wore a wide-brimmed hat to ward off the heat. I understand why cowboys wear cowboy hats — protection from a sun that feels piercing.

Some Austinites leave over the summer, to escape the heat. But summer is my favorite season here: Cicadas. Swimming holes. Water parks. Afternoons in the neighborhood pool. The odd way I have to carry a light sweater around to protect me from the overly air-conditioned interiors. The lemon and eucalyptus oil I use on my skin to ward off mosquitoes.

My work schedule doesn't change, but I still call these days "lazy days." It's the heat, my slower run times, the way I bask by the pool's edge.

Summer means traveling, exploring small-town Texas, camping.

Not having to pack school lunches in the morning.

Smoothies, slushies, ice cream.

Swimming at the Micki Krebsbach pool and eating Round Rock Donuts.

Or staring out of the bedroom window at 8:30 p.m., watching the sunset.

But more than anything, summer means unexpected plans, new discoveries, and waking up excited to meet the day.

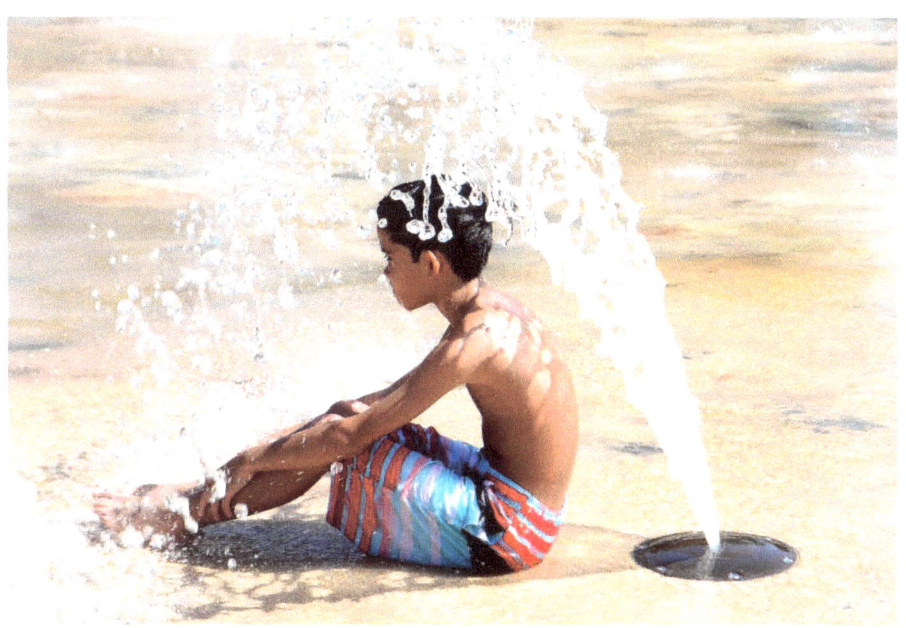

Still, I'd be a fool not to notice that Austin is getting hotter. Last year, in 2023, there were three straight months of 100+ degree weather. The summer of 2023 was apparently the hottest weather the Northern Hemisphere experienced in more than 2,000 years, according to a study in the *Nature* journal.

Surprisingly, the steaming hot weather doesn't bother me. But it's hard on our air conditioner and our bills.

We try to balance our usage, turning it on only when necessary. However, with two other people in the house who struggle with heat more than I do, this is a challenge.

When we're on vacation, one of the first questions people ask me is, "How do you stand the heat there?"

I just do. Our bodies get used to it, like everything else.

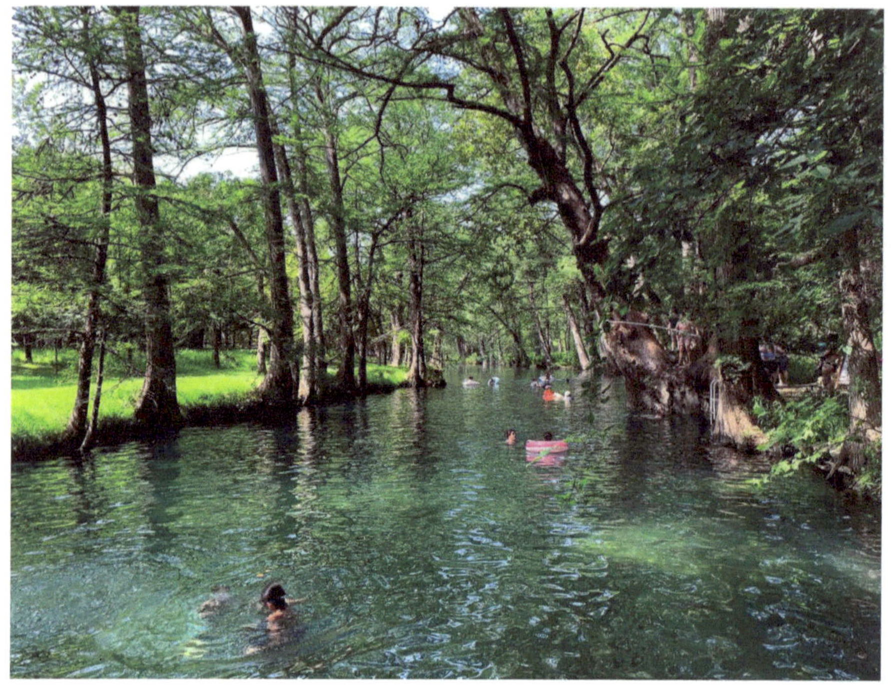

Wimberley Blue Hole

Swimming Holes

Every summer, I step into a Huckleberry Finn novel. Cypress trees hug the water, their roots splay out along the river's edge, and lines of people swing from ropes. This is summer at its best.

We're lucky.

The increasing heat waves and the rising temperatures mean Texas's swimming holes are dwindling.

And as writer Joe Nick Patoski wrote in the Texas Monthly magazine, "By 2005, only 17 of the 31 large springs once known in Texas remained."

It's 2023, and for two years straight, Jacob's Well has been closed due to low water levels.

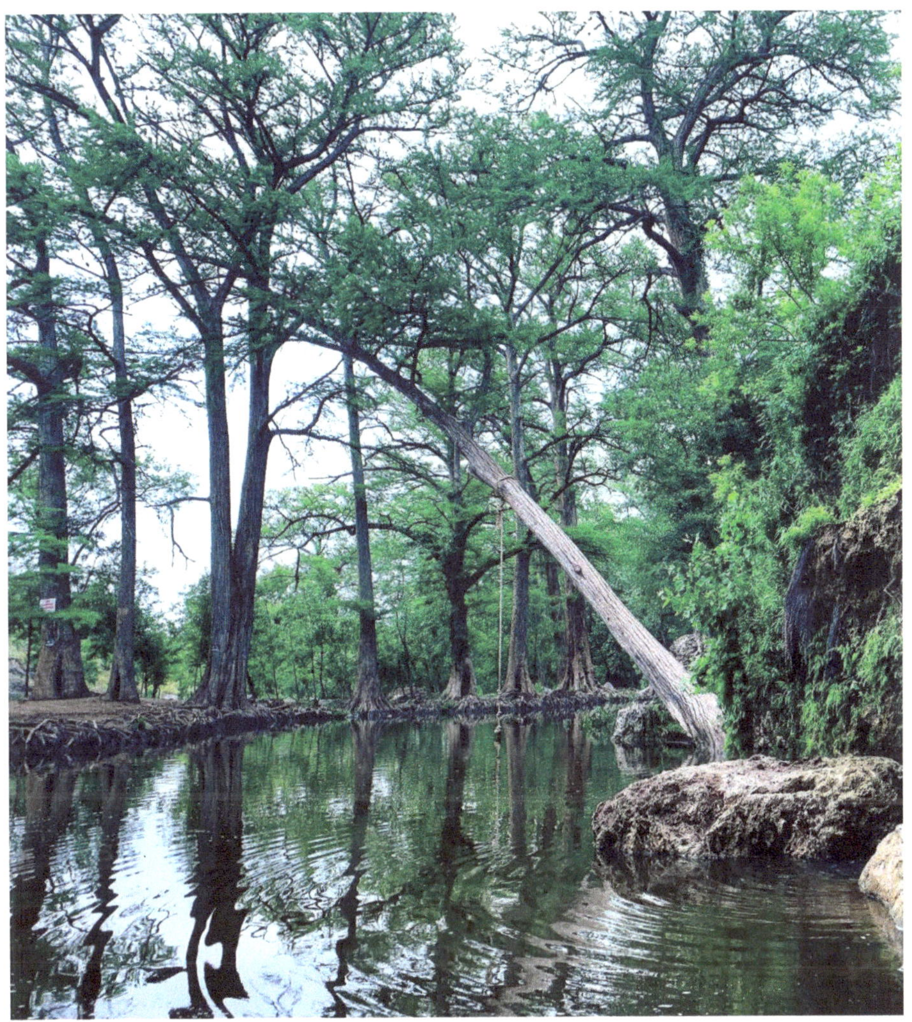

Krause Springs

The other day, I looked down at the Blanco River from our restaurant in Wimberley. It was dry... mostly. And there was a short-lived fear that our Blue Hole reservation would be canceled. The Blue Hole was fine, though. Cool water. Refreshing. Crowded. Breathtaking.

But that day will come.

For now, my routine is the same. I watch my son swing off the rope. I wade in my water shoes, slowly inching deeper into the water. I float along the river in my tube. And every year, I say the same thing.

We're lucky.

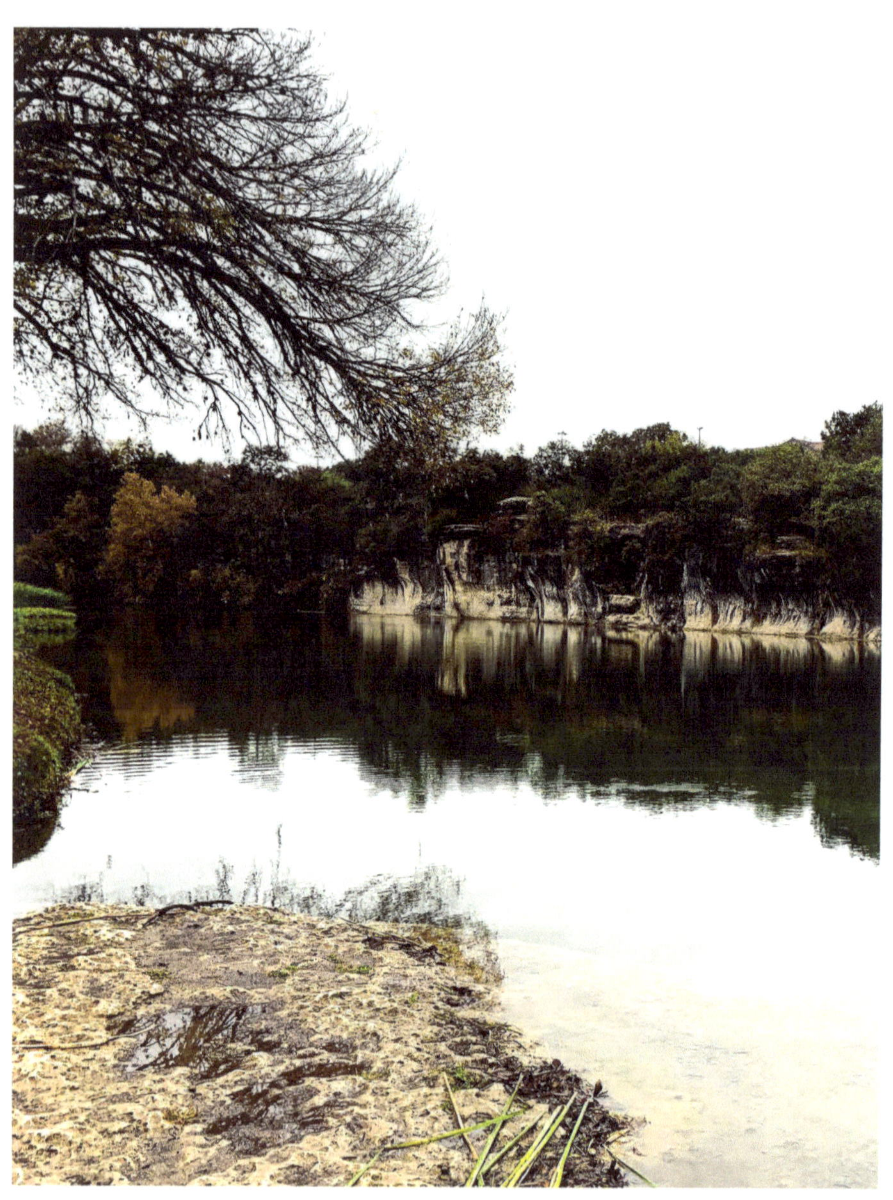

Blue Hole in Georgetown

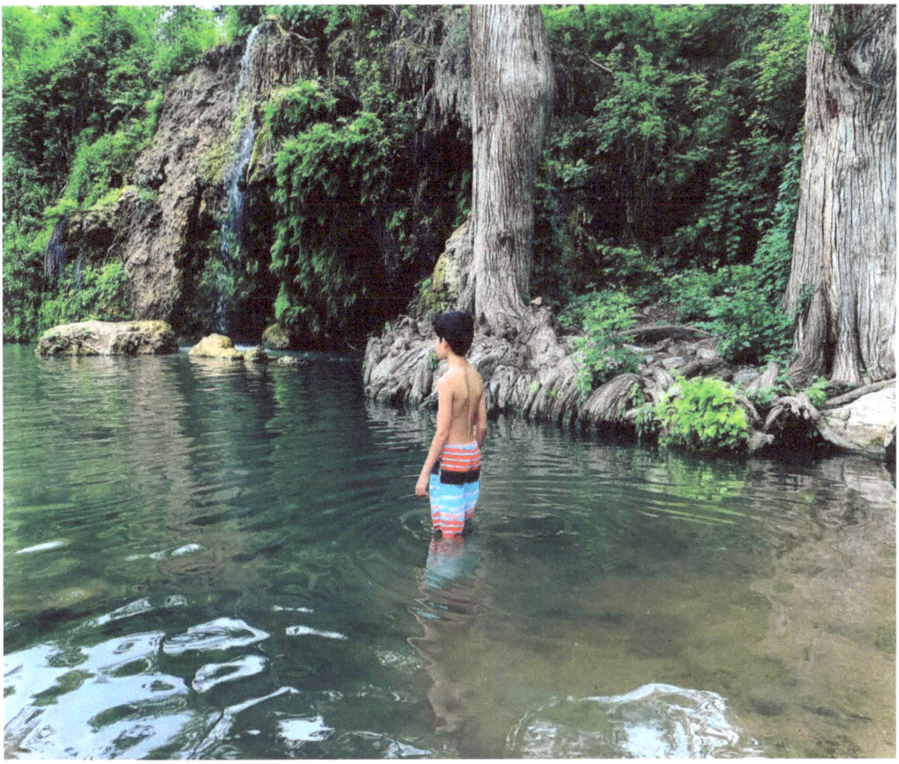

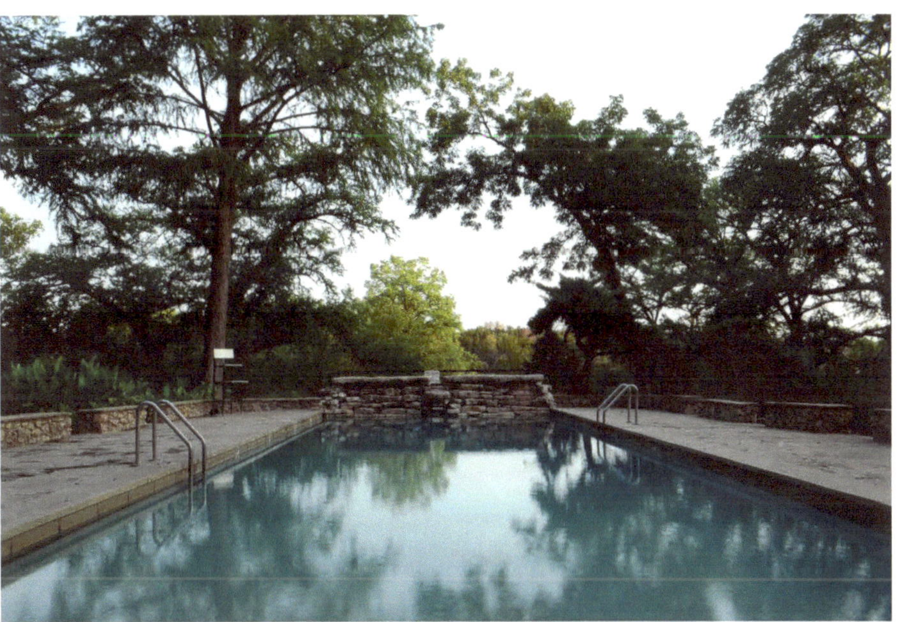

Our "Garden of Eden" campsite - Krause Springs

The spring-fed pool at Krause Springs

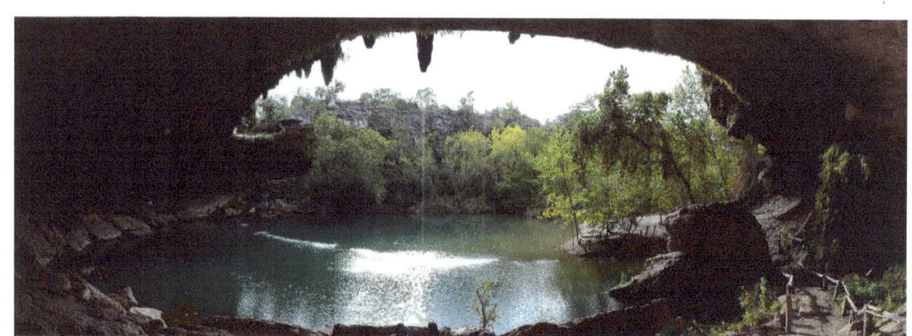

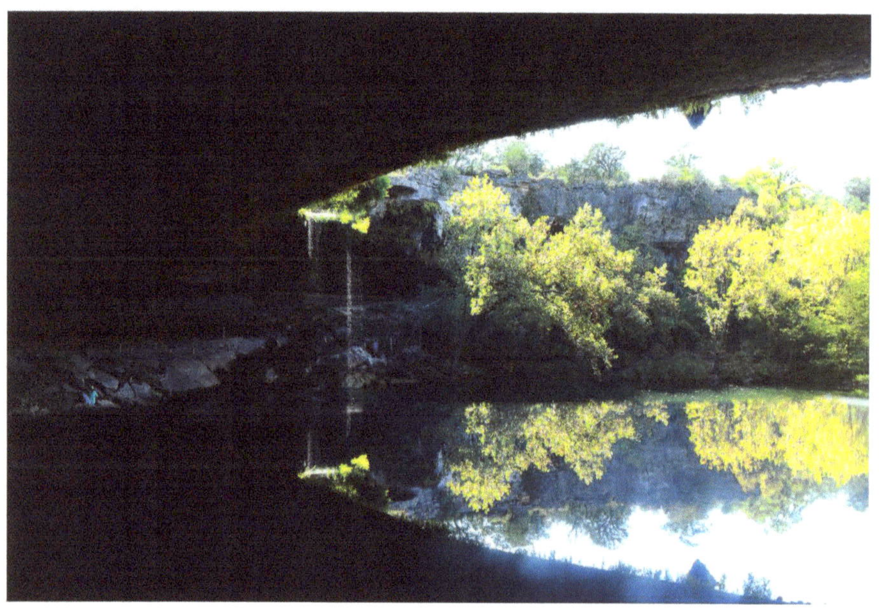

Hamilton Pool

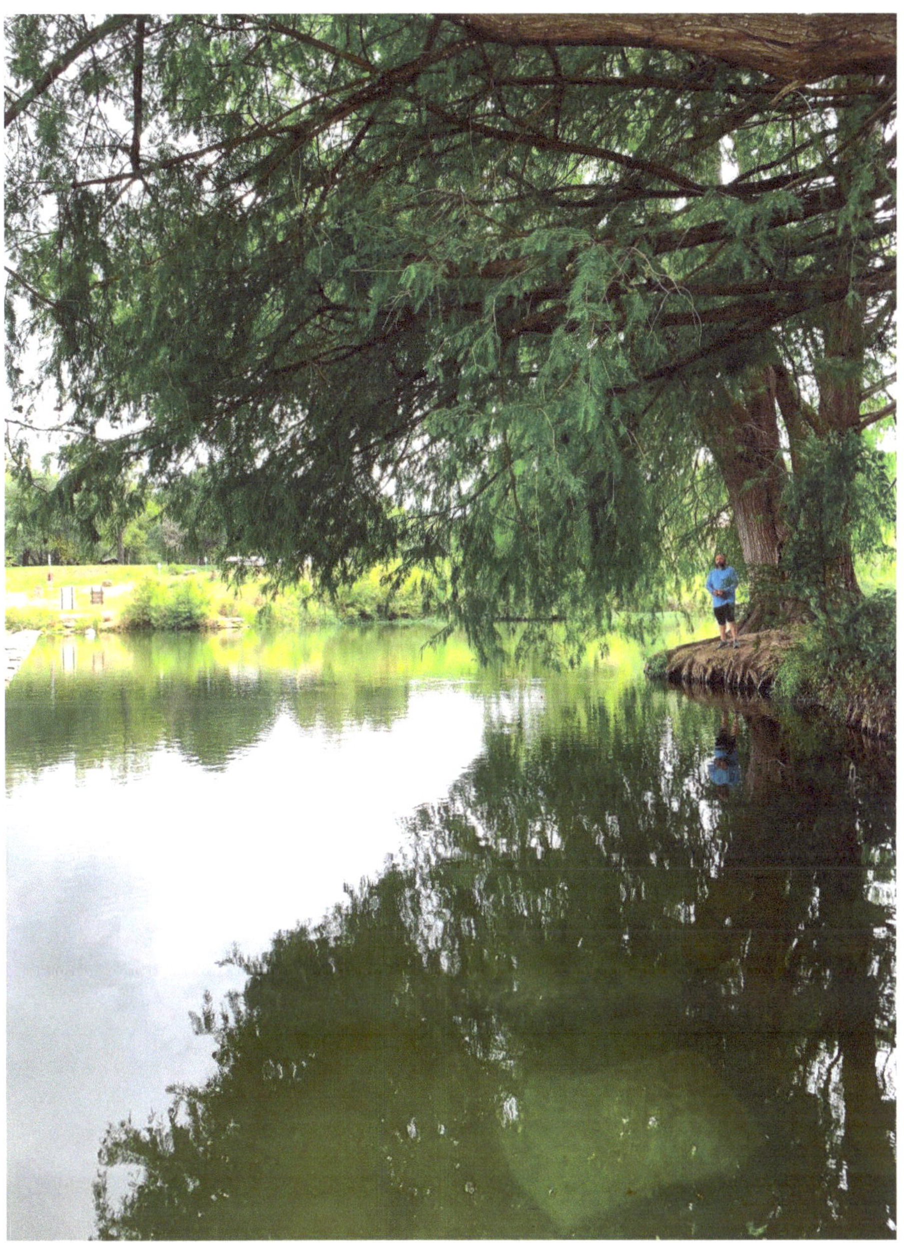

Blanco State Park

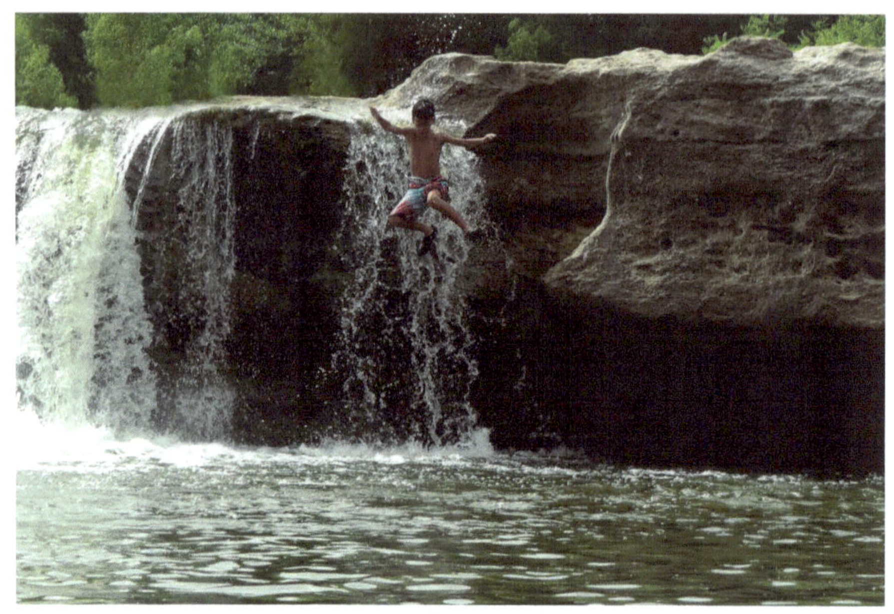

McKinney Falls State Park

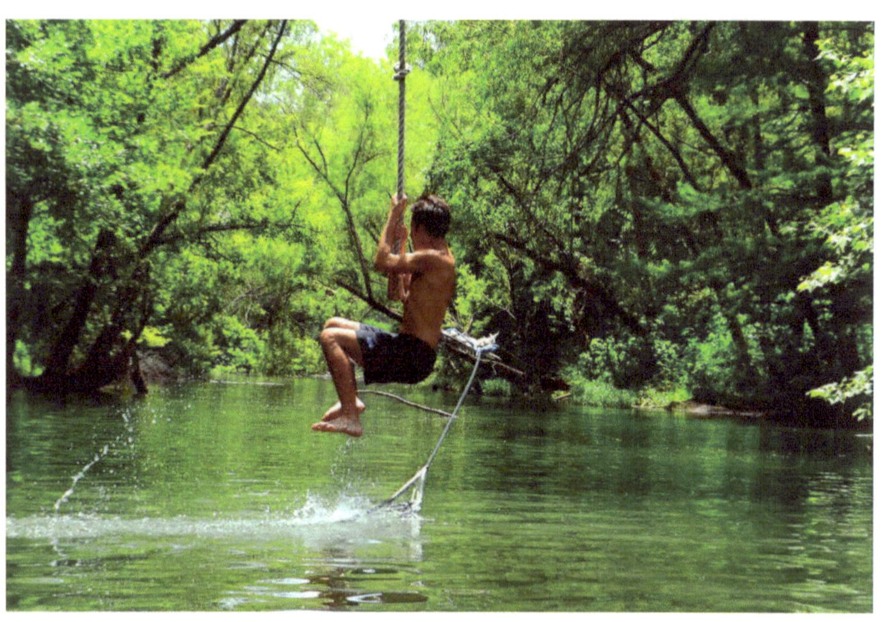

St. Edward's Park Swimming Hole

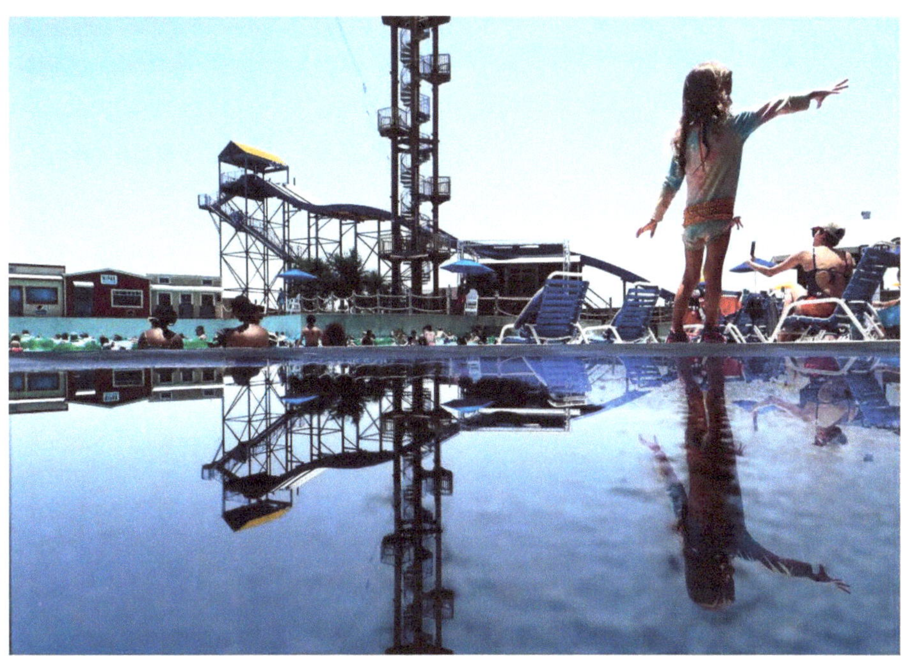

Typhoon Texas

Childhood & Water Parks

Water parks. An alternative to swimming holes. This is where we come to cool off from the heat. Weather so hot, the news says it's hotter than 99% of the world.

My time at water parks is limited. It's carefree and happy. And it means childhood - my son's.

I take photos all the time, knowing I'll look back at them wistfully ... remembering. The Lazy River. The Tidal Wave Bay. The Gully Washer.

I don't bring books or magazines because I want to be fully present so I can say: I was here. With him.

Years of water parks and theme parks mean watching him grow and change, watching his childhood, and proudly being part of it.

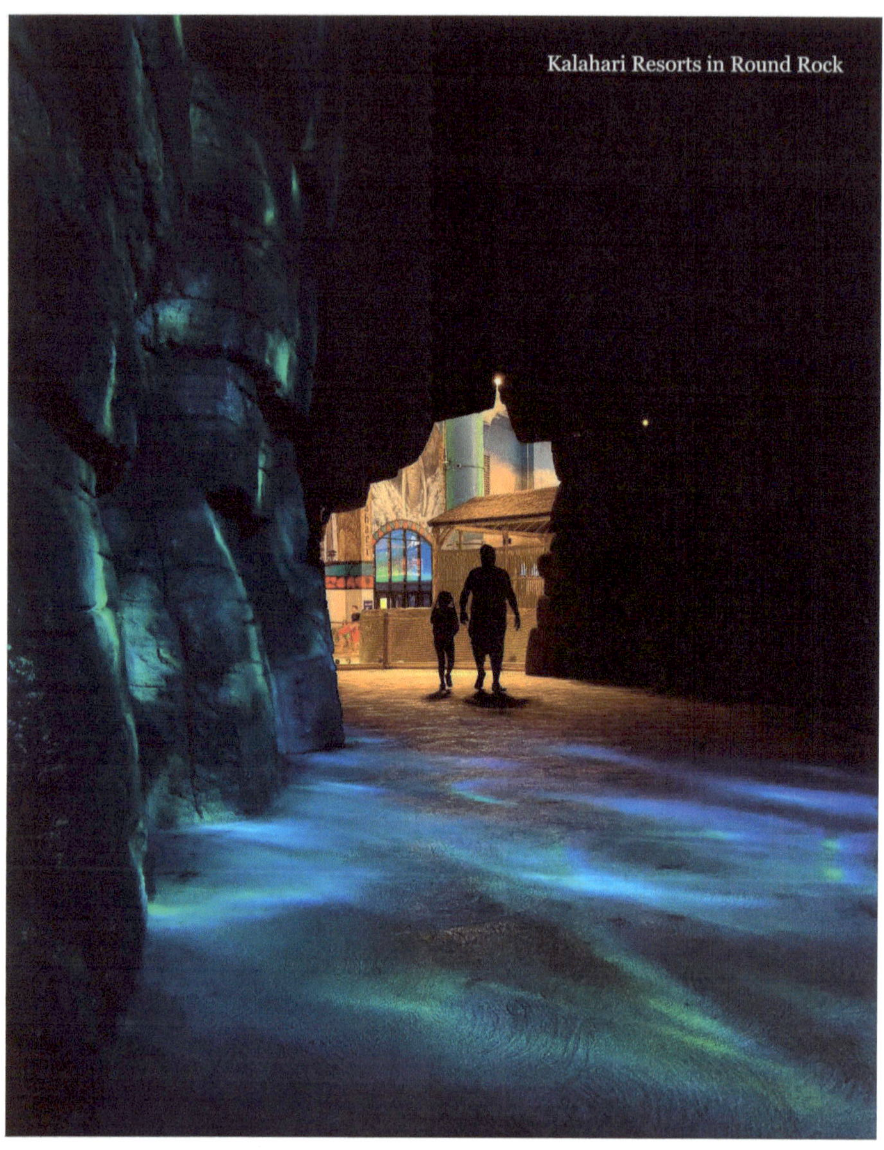

Almost as soon as I finish writing this, his interest in water parks wanes, putting an abrupt end to exploring water parks in Texas.

I want to tell him that we still haven't explored Schlitterbahn thoroughly, but I catch myself. Going to water parks isn't about me. It's a childhood gift that he's outgrown.

These are the times I'll remember, though: the moments I saw his childhood disappear, almost evaporate like vapor. Or maybe I should say: the moments I was lucky enough to see him growing up.

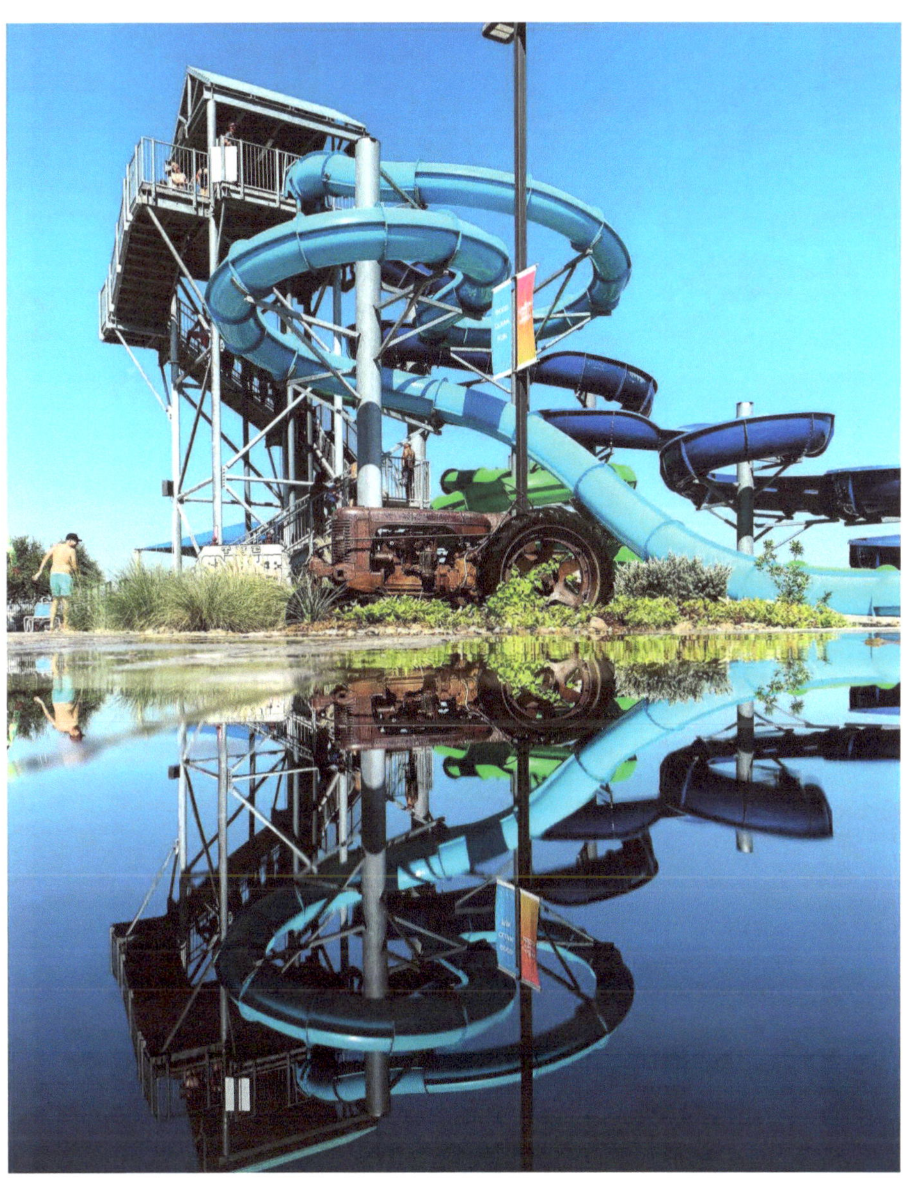

Typhoon Texas

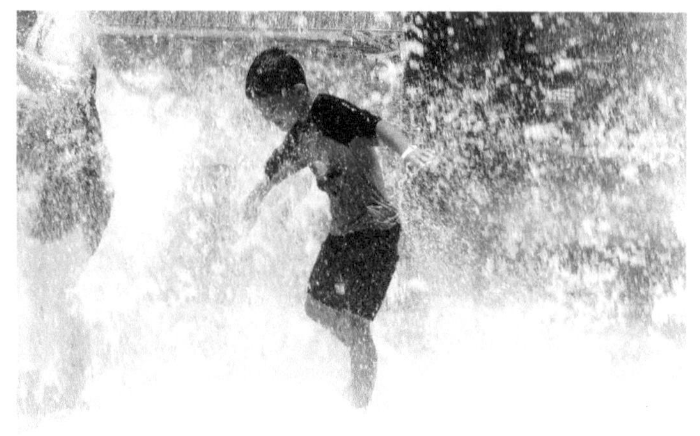

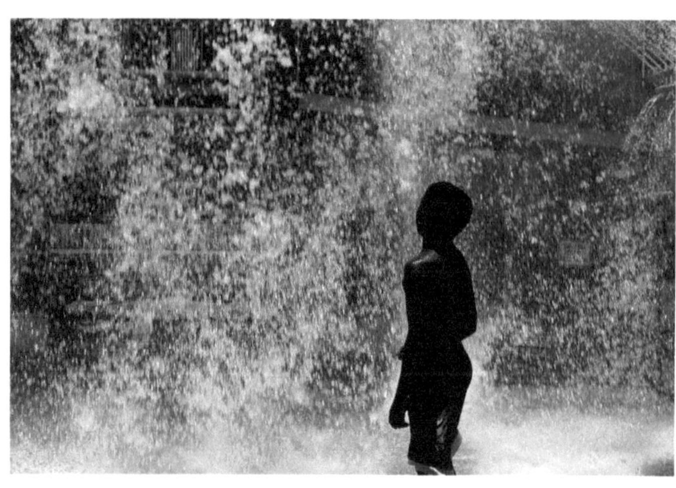

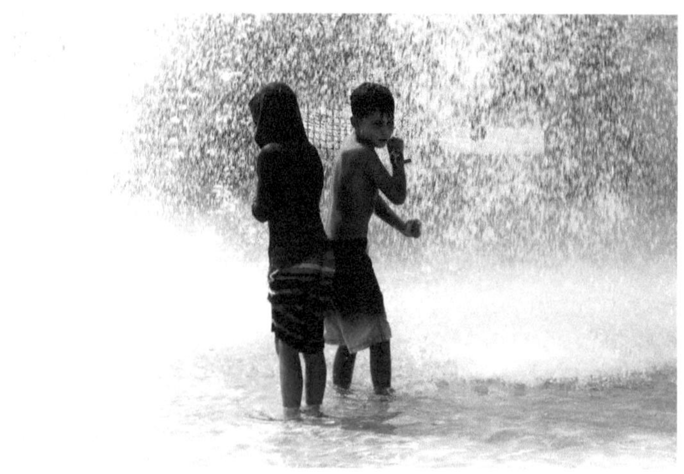

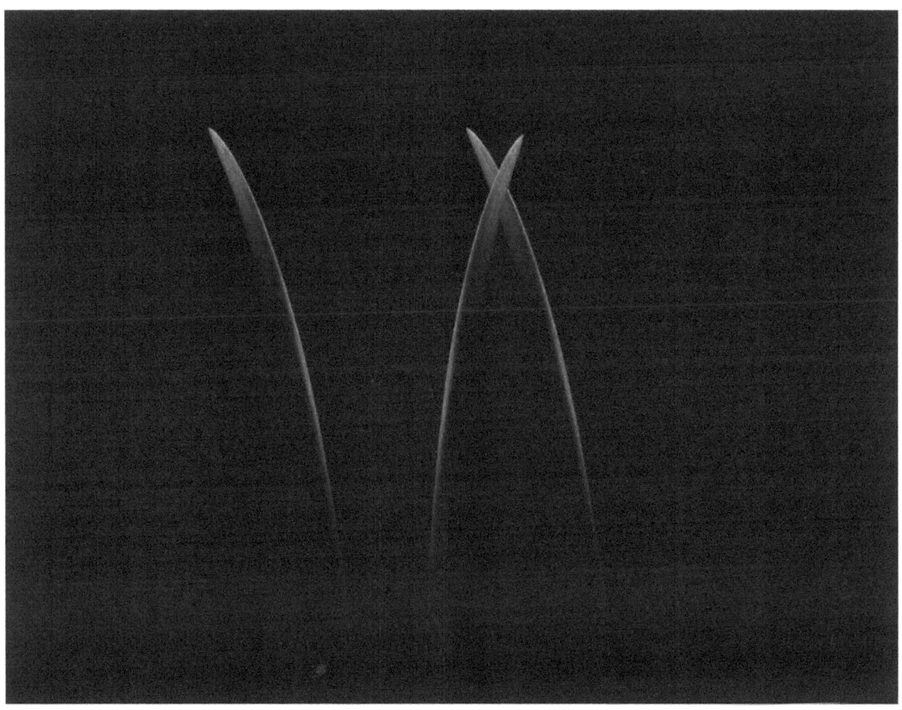

"A lawn is nature under totalitarian rule" - Michael Pollan

HEAT WAVES

When we're not in water, we're in air-conditioned interiors. Our electricity bill soars. Fans, alone, won't do the job, making air conditioning a necessity - there are 100+ degree temperatures week after week.

Our grass fizzles, turning yellow then brown. I don't worry about the back yard, but the front yard demands care. It's lawn etiquette and suburban upkeep. But it's also a waste of water.

A CNN report shows "keeping front lawn grass alive requires up to 75% of just one household's water consumption."

Nevada has recently outlawed all grass lawns. A new Las Vegas law requires homeowners to get rid of their lawns by 2027. And Scottsdale, AZ, has banned natural grass in front yards of new homes.

I hope Austin will take equally radical steps. Austin is at the forefront with tiny homes, technology, the LGBTQ community.

Maybe prohibiting non-functional grass on front lawns will be next.

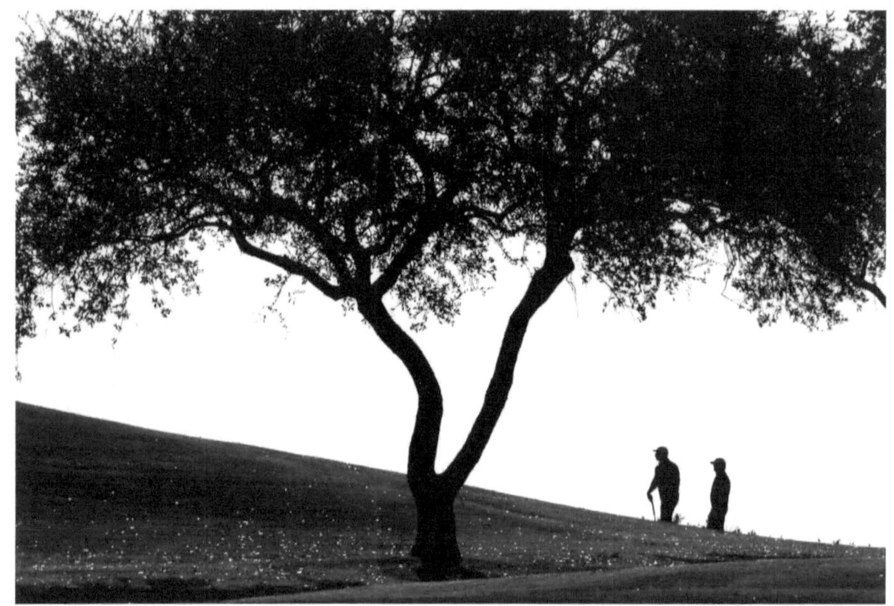

Wednesday mornings. My jogging route takes me past our neighborhood golf course, and I watch the sprinklers spray the lush grass. The water is a combination of reclaimed water and Trinity Aquifer water. The latter supplies drinking water to the Texas Hill County.

Should our drinking water supply compete with water for golf courses?

I question, I judge, but I'm guilty, too. My son took golf classes for five years, playing on 9-hole and 18-hole golf courses and hitting golf balls on grass that was spongy and green.

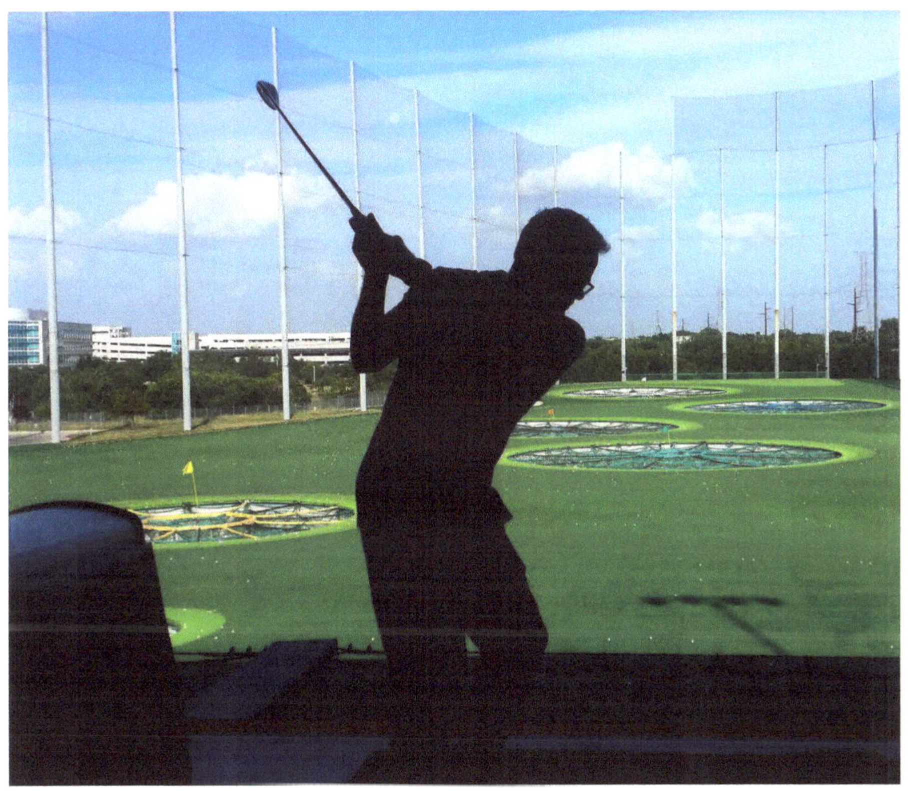

TopGolf in Austin

Now that I have to water my front lawn during an extended heat wave, I think about water waste all the time, though.

Recycled or reclaimed water. These words pop up often, and I see more golf courses making a 100% switch. I applaud their efforts to adapt: TopGolf Austin's 13-acre outdoor driving range uses artificial turf instead of real grass.

But are golf courses living on borrowed time?

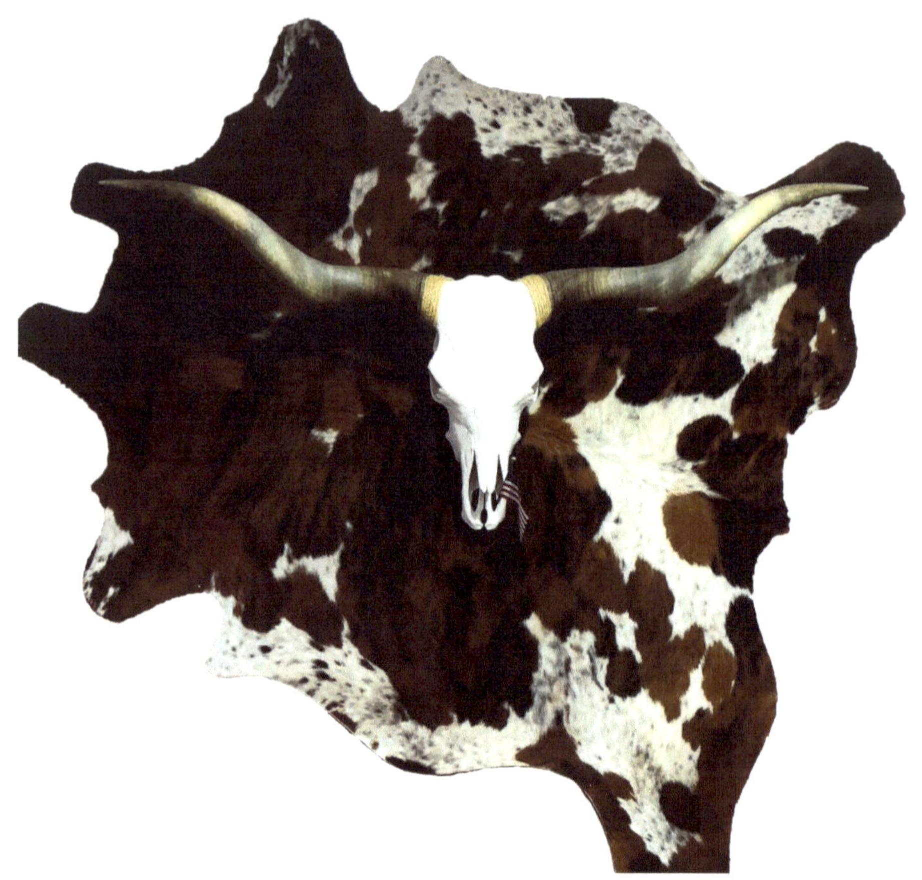

The Republic of BBQs, Tacos, & Tex-Mex

Cyclone Ayana.
Then there was a name change: Valencia's Tex-Mex Garage.
Then it shuttered its doors.

Cyclone Ayana was our first Text-Mex restaurant, and our first meal at a restaurant in Austin. It was also our first restaurant outing after the pandemic. I was a little heartbroken to see it go.

One of the best ways to discover a city is through its food.

- What the locals eat and why
- The evolution of Tex-Mex cuisine
- Why BBQ in small-town Texas never seems to come with fries
- How the best peach cobbler is served in the peach capital, Fredericksburg
- And why pecan pies are as authentic to Texas as cowboys

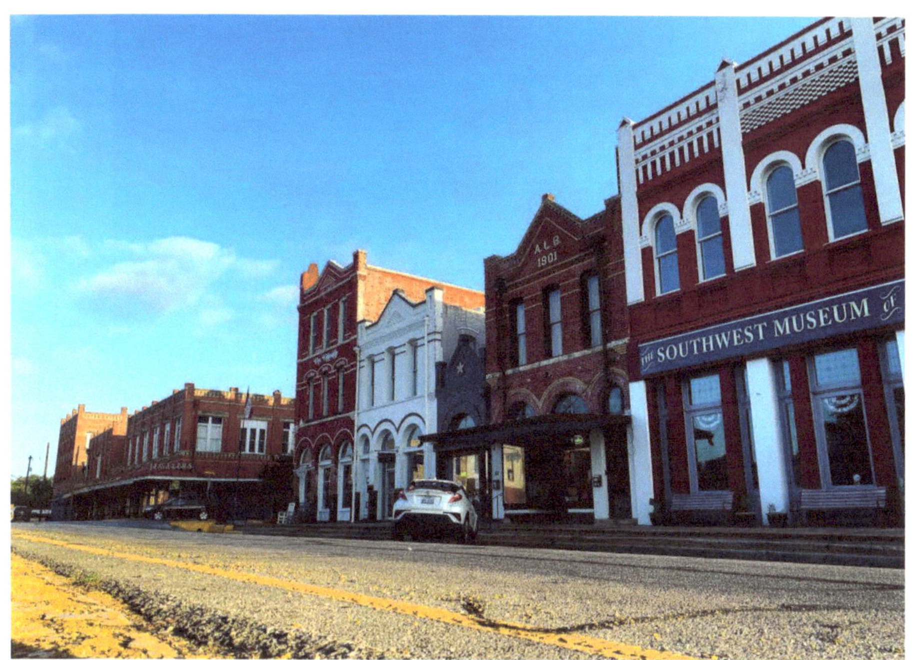
Downtown Lockhart

Austin's signature dishes are tacos (breakfast tacos), Tex-Mex (with queso), and brisket BBQ.

The debates are endless: where to get the best of each and who outshines whom. There's even a BBQ club: TM BBQ Club for Texans who "really, really, *really* love BBQ." Members get to attend members-only "meat-ups," get early access to BBQ Fest tickets, receive discounts at BBQ restaurants, purchase BBQ merch, and more.

Texans love their BBQ.

They may be justified. Texas Monthly's barbecue editor, Daniel Vaughn, declares that Texas barbecue has become the "definitive barbecue style of America."

I'm not a member of any BBQ club, but I do have my favorite spots, just like everyone else who lives here. The best BBQ is the moist and fatty brisket BBQ at The Original Black's Barbecue, 45 minutes south of Austin in Lockhart, the BBQ capital of Texas. (Others may disagree.)

Tacos: Our neighborhood food truck.

And Tex-Mex: I'm still looking. (Though Torchy Tacos came in at #2 on USA Today's "10 Best Fast Casual Restaurants" list in 2024.)

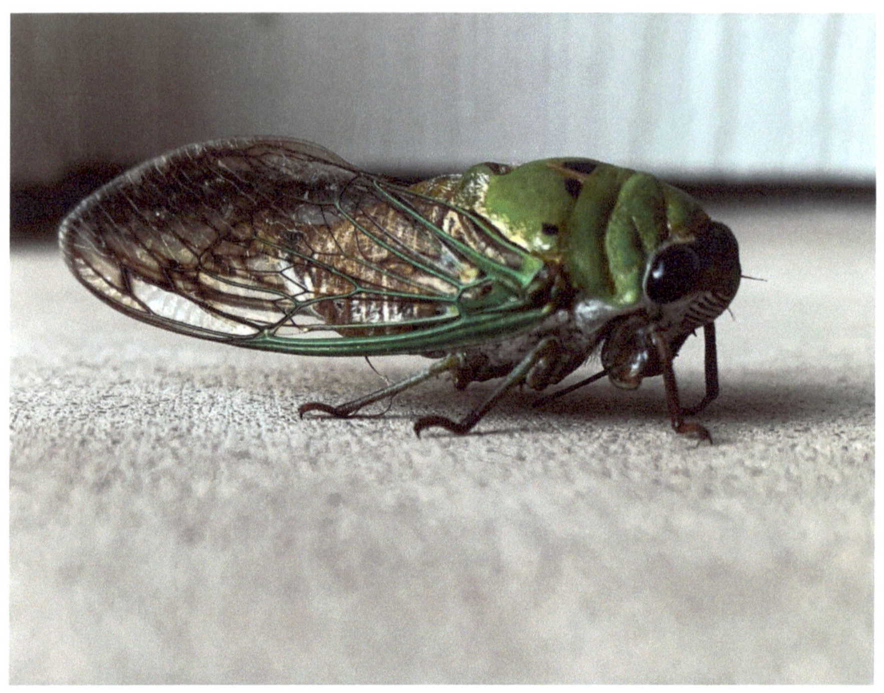

Dog Day Cicadas

I like the way he looks at me. And even though I can't quite make out where he's looking, I know his eyes are tracking my every move.

I approach cautiously, snapping photos from every angle. He remains motionless. I know if I touch him or poke him with a stick, his wings will flutter or he'll hop backwards. But I don't want to. I enjoy our impromptu photoshoot.

This will be a sad ending ... for him. He landed on my doorstep to die. Dog day cicadas have a lifespan of about 2-5 years and then live for roughly 2-6 weeks after mating. Once they fall to the ground, their mating is complete and death is near.

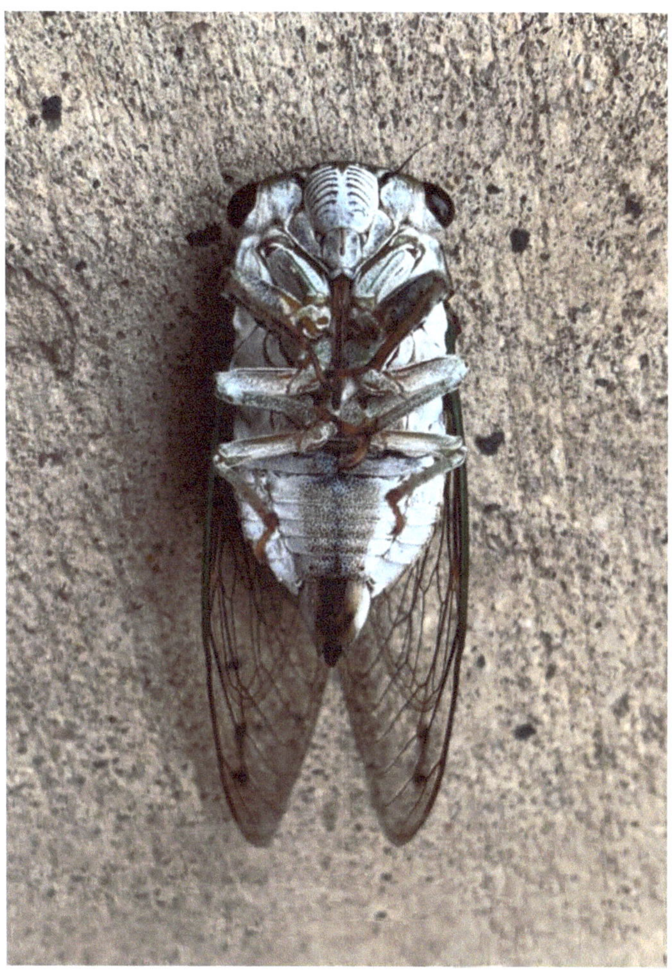

My first introduction to cicadas was a brown husk stuck to our garbage can. It startled me. I may have even leaped back in fear. After I poked and prodded it and realized it was just a shell, I went online to do some research, intrigued.

Adult cicadas emerge from their nymph stage and leave their shells behind. In our case, they leave their abandoned husks on our garden shed and garbage cans.

I find lots of cicadas on the ground over the summer: lying on their back with their white bellies exposed, half-eaten, or still somewhat alert. They look like alien insects that fell from another planet, quietly dying in the searing heat.

Which is why I begin to collect them, stare at them, take photos of them, and study them.

In early 2024, I was thrilled to learn that two cicada broods would emerge over the summer: Brood XIII and Brood XIX. There would be twice the number of cicadas and twice the racket. But when I re-read the article, I learned the cicadas would only emerge in the Midwest and the Southeast.

I was disappointed, to say the least. Texas would only get its usual one: our dog day cicada.

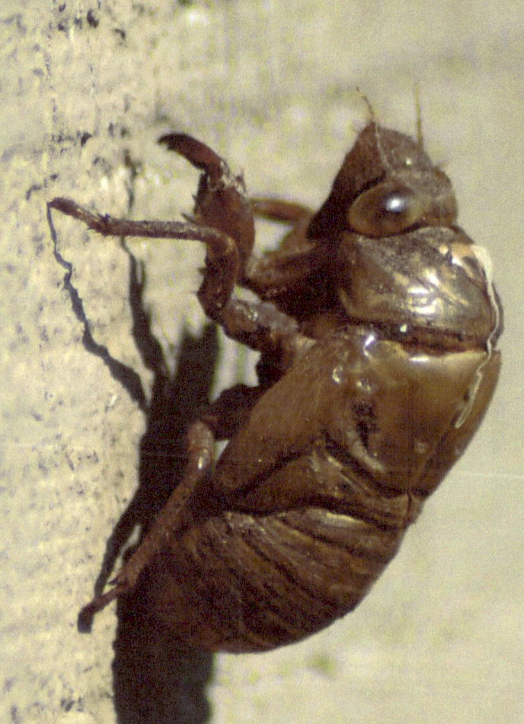

I collect so many dead cicadas and their empty husks — storing them in clear plastic bags — that I no longer know what to do with them. They collect on my desk, next to my batch of pens. A makeshift, plastic mortuary.

In the end, as the days get shorter, I complete their journey and return them to the soil in our garden. It's a quiet end to a thunderous, fleeting life.

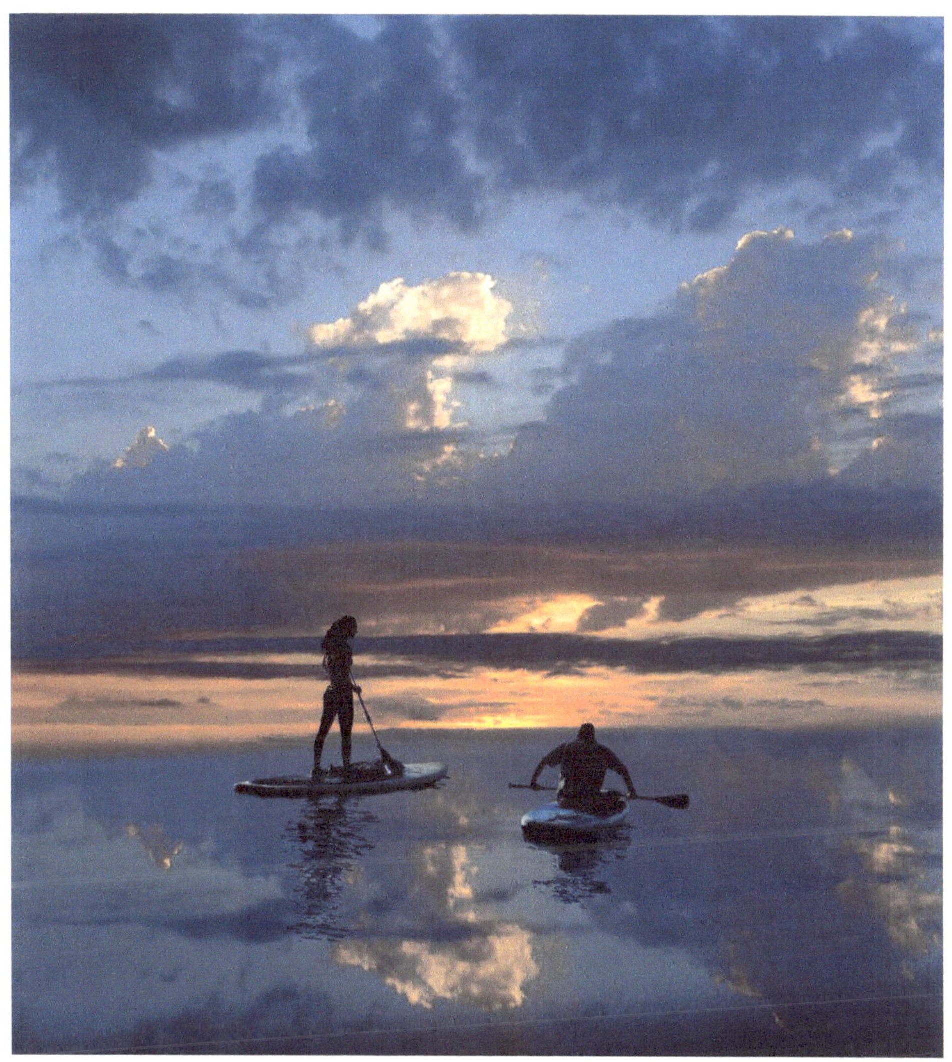

The End of Summer

Earlier sunsets. Dead cicadas. My son flopping on my bed, bored. Summer activities ticked off.

We've done everything I scheduled. International vacation. Check. Camping. Check. Swimming holes. Check. Waterparks. Check. Restaurants and summer movies. Check.

And now we wait. For the new school year. For cooler weather. For fall.

The last two weeks, I leave the weekends empty. A psychological preparation for the upcoming year. But this translates to boredom. Lots of it.

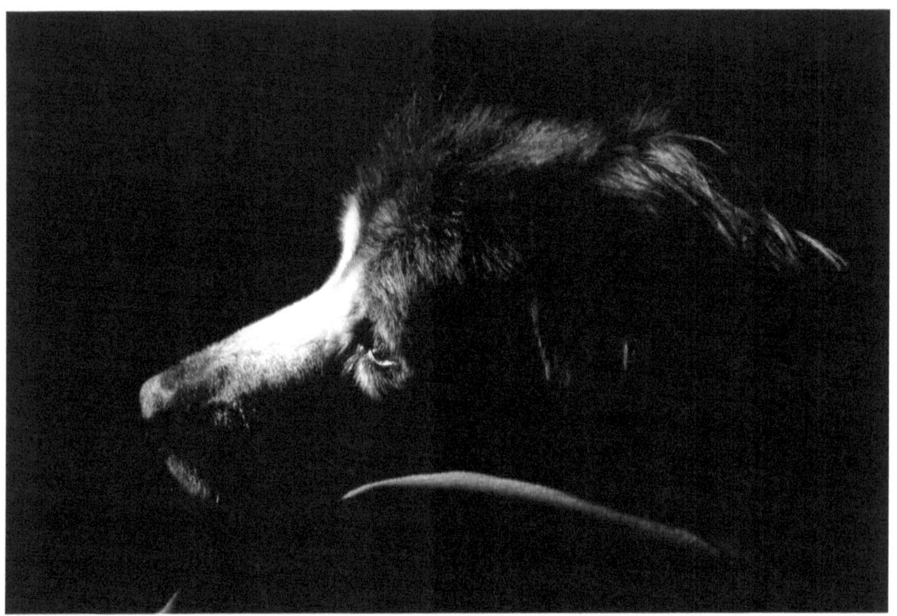

The summer heat still engulfs us, and my dog walks around the house, lethargic. Even with our AC on, it's like she can feel the heat seeping in from under the doors. I walk her less — it's usually too hot for her paws. So like the rest of us, boredom sets in. And we lay around the house, staring at screens.

As my son gets older, these final two weeks are punctuated by driving lessons and hours upon hours at the rock climbing gym. Interiors seem to beckon us more.

Towards the end of summer, short bursts of rain puncture our blanket of heat. The respite is brief, and temperatures drop for a few hours.

But we finally get a taste of what's coming.

UNTITLED AND NAMELESS

I didn't want to write this, but I have to. Not for me. For them.

I shy away from local news. It's a detailed obituary page, a listing of who died in the city. Car accidents. Domestic violence. Armed robberies. Police shootings.

Which means I don't find out about the news by reading. My son tells me. His phone pinged while he was in school.

We're desensitized now, as a city and as a country. But this incident haunts me for weeks.

Aug 31st, 2023. The location: our favorite slushie cafe. Number of deaths: three, including the shooter.

I'm research-oriented, so I immerse myself in details. The shooter is educated. But his LinkedIn page shows two failed startups. There's a year of silence. Then the shooting.

Academic excellence. A failed career. Nothing built. And then selfish violence to make headlines, to gain the notoriety that had alluded him in life. This is a guess. It's the only way I can make sense of it.

Only one victim's name comes up. I research her, too. Well-traveled. Intelligent. A career in tech. The last 12 years, she owned a boutique hotel abroad.

I let my research consume me because I need to know she was loved, had a full life, was content. A few days later, the local news station does a video tribute. Her friends speak of her glowingly.

It's not enough, but it's something. An acknowledgment from the community that she had value, that we lost someone special.

I choose not to include a photo here. Going to the scene of the crime to revisit our boarded-up slushie cafe would have felt voyeuristic, disrespectful.

I leave a blank page instead. For her. For all the past victims. For the future ones.

It's my own small tribute.

Fall

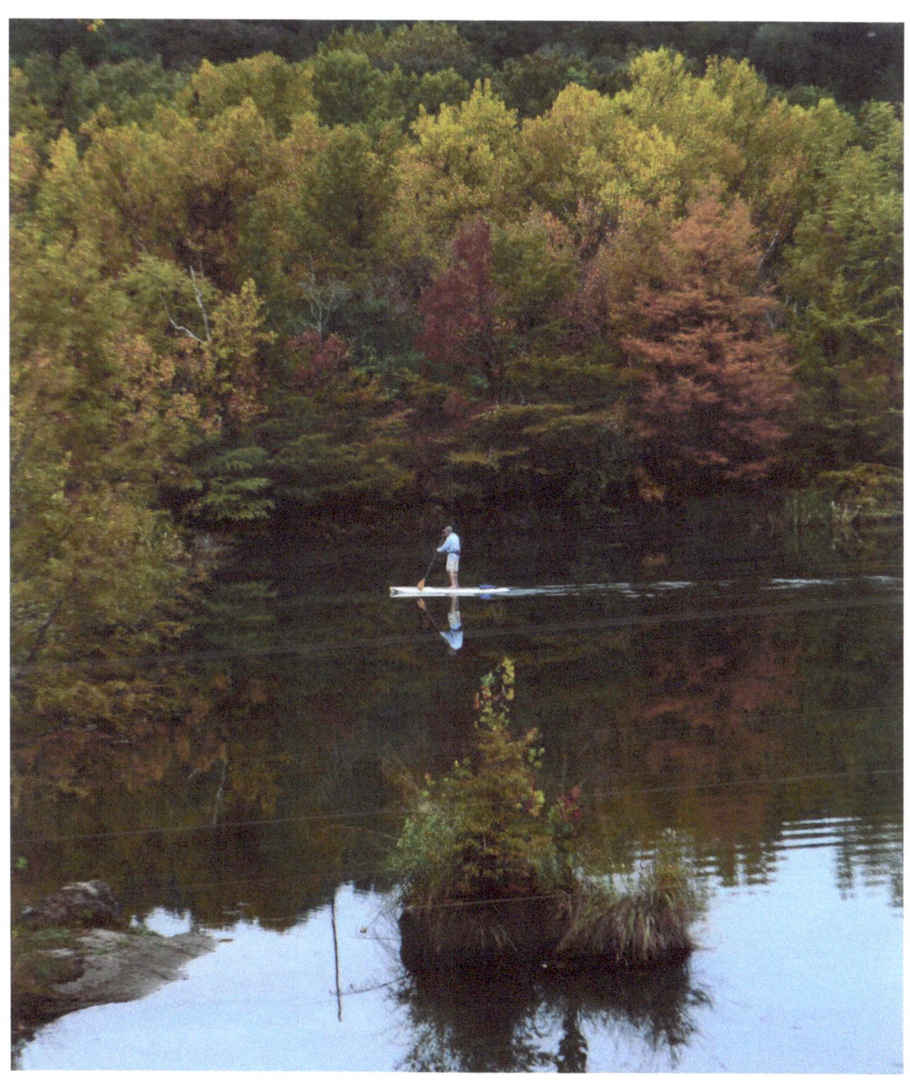

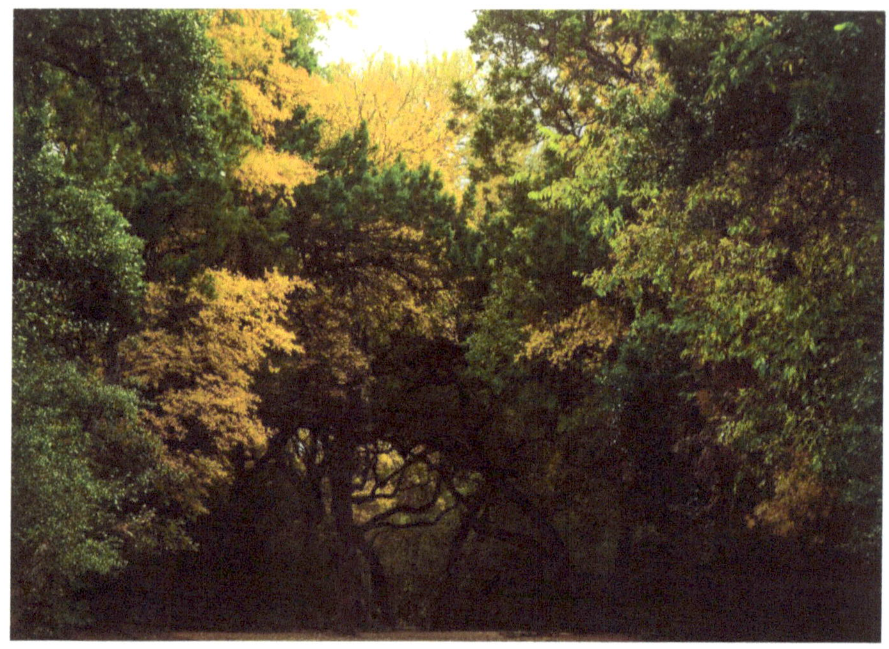

The rain woke me up. Large sheets of water and lightning that felt like blue strobe lights. The rain has washed some of the heat away, and for the first time in three months, the AC is off and the windows are open. It's 3:27 a.m. and the air is still a little humid. I don't mind.

Fall. We are one week away, and the refreshing rain and slight dip in temperatures say we're inching closer.

I make a list of the things I can do now:

— Turn off the AC
— Open our windows
— Walk the dog earlier now that the pavement doesn't burn her paws
— Eat in the garden
— Wear a light sweater
— Drink warm tea in the afternoon
—Watch the leaves turn to burnt orange, red, or brown

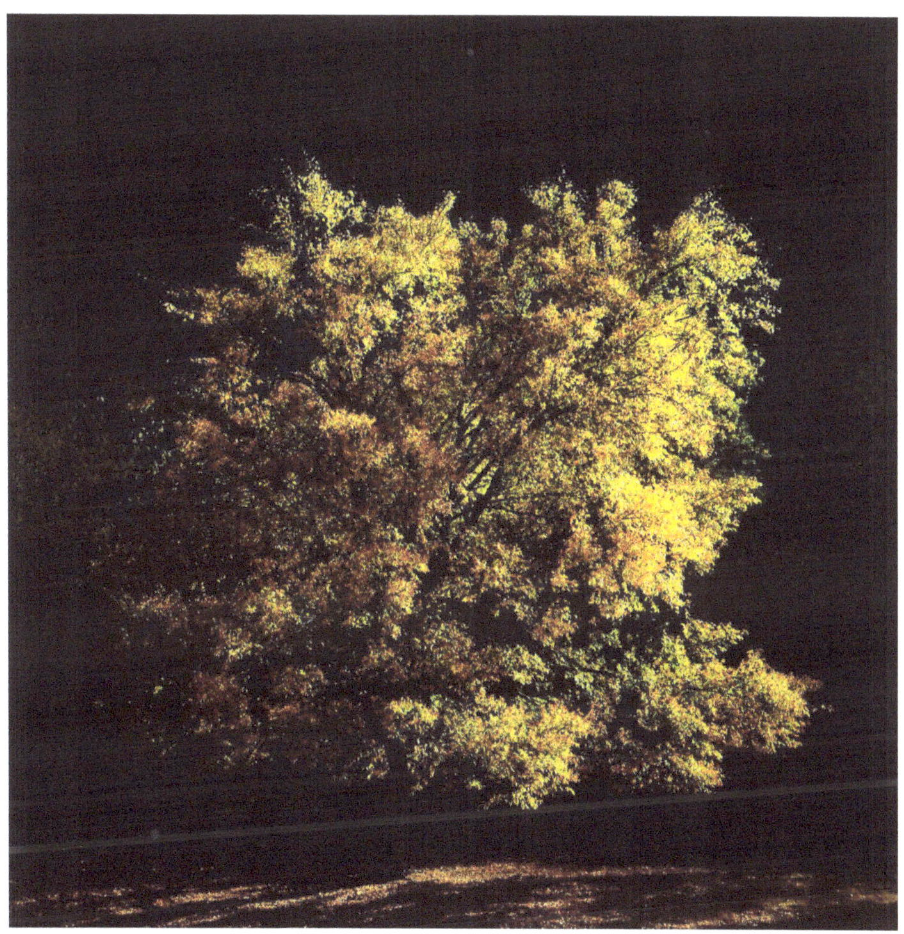

The transition to fall isn't smooth. The weather flip flops. It's 46 degrees Fahrenheit this morning, and I'm wearing two layers of clothing as well as a beanie for my morning walk. My hands don't go numb, but they're cold.

Three days from now, it will be 93 degrees.

The supermarket and the movie theater didn't get the memo. They're freezing inside, with temperatures set somewhere to around 65 degrees. I shiver when I shop. I bring a blanket (and sweater) to the movie theater.

The back and forth takes its toll, and my body struggles to adjust.

Fall in Austin begins differently for everyone. For me, it begins with a cold. Add on sweaters, soups, and herbal teas.

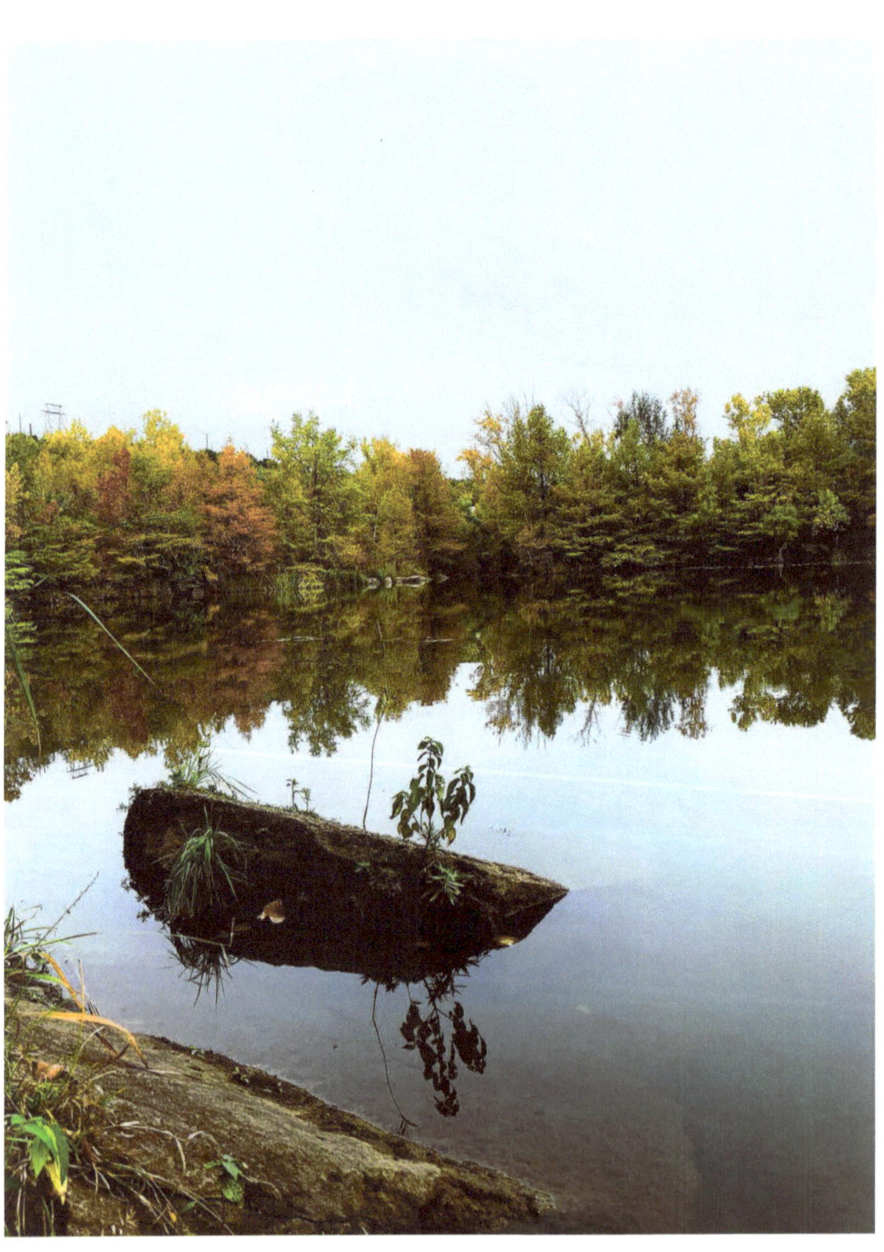

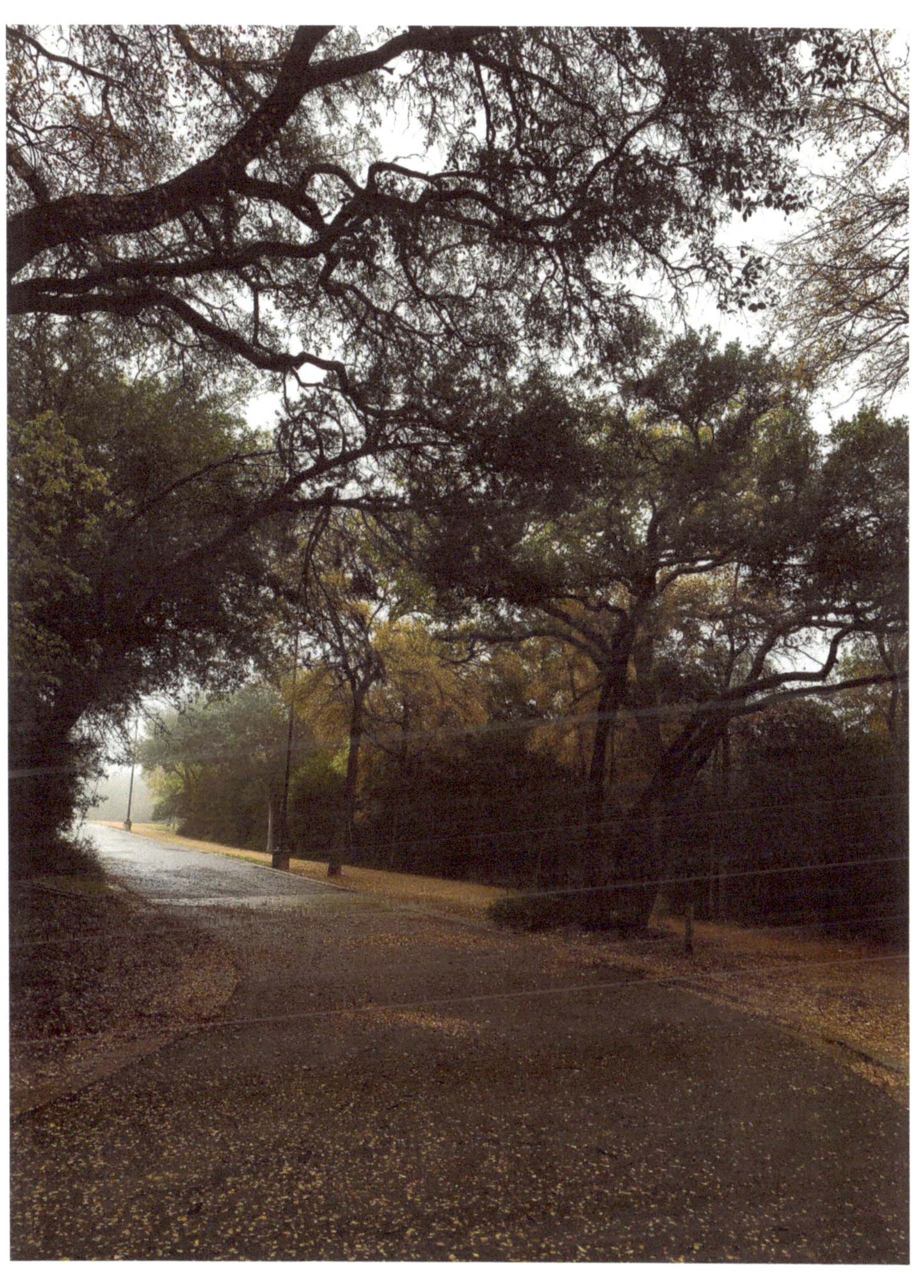

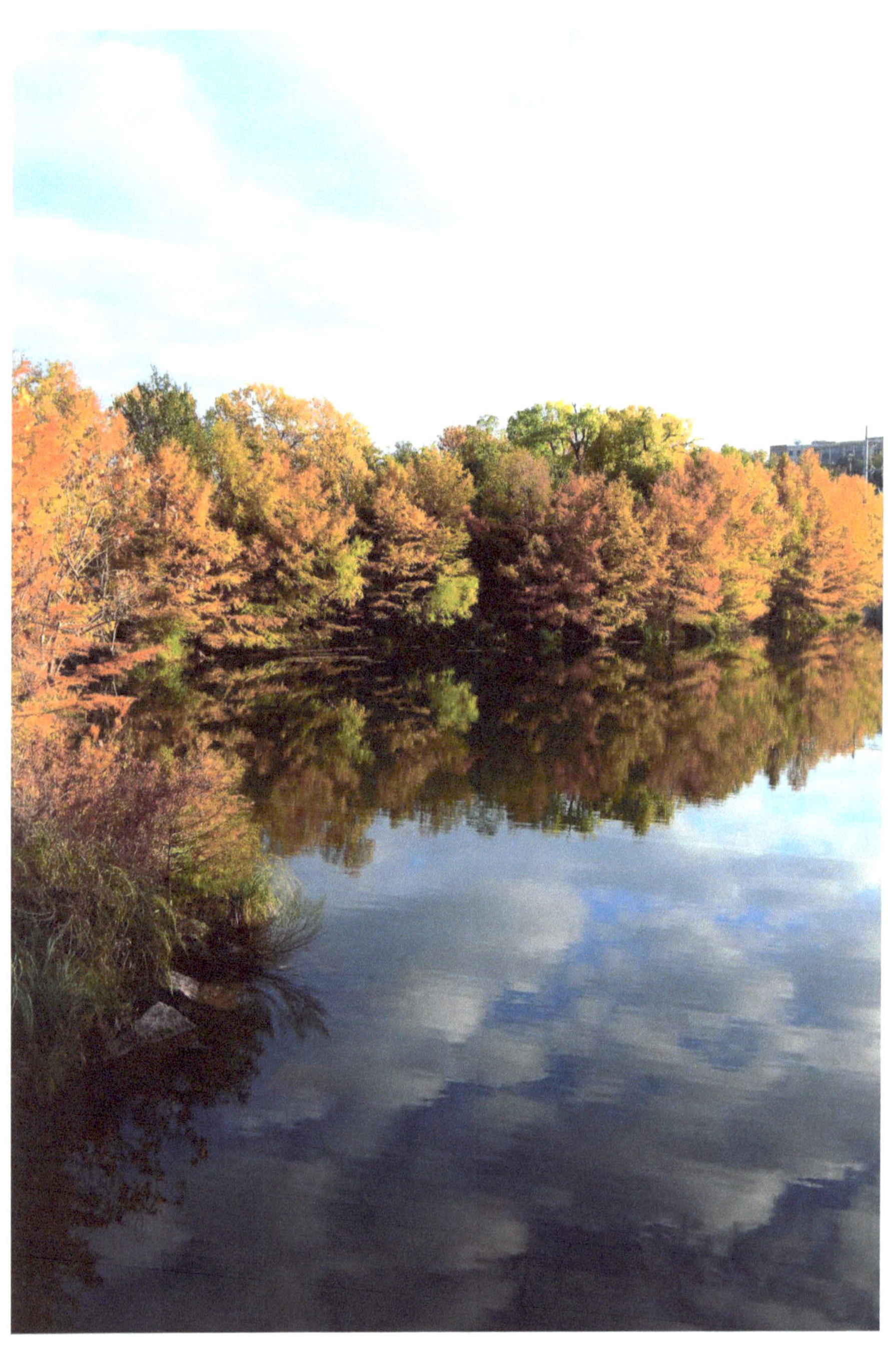

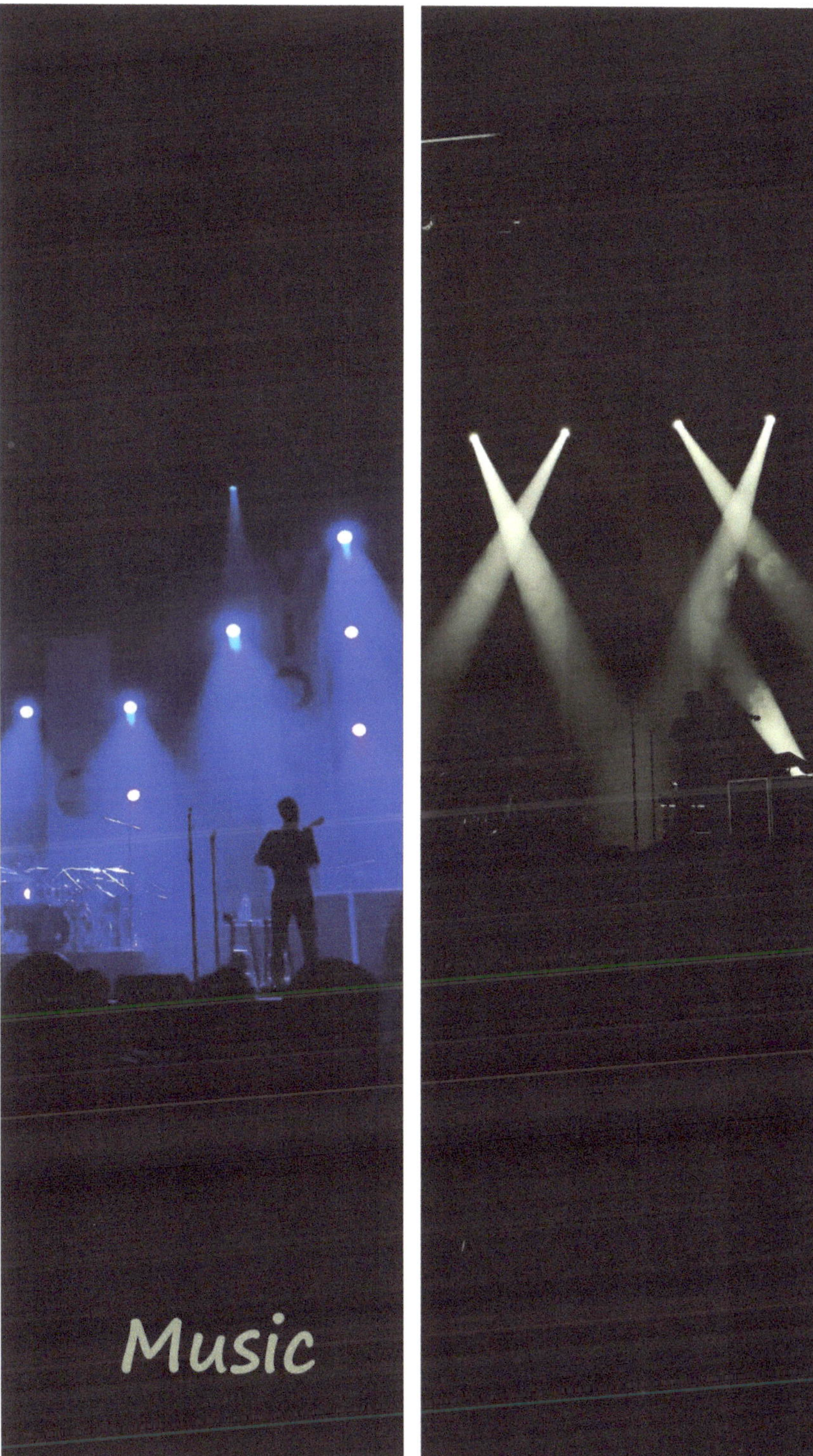
Music

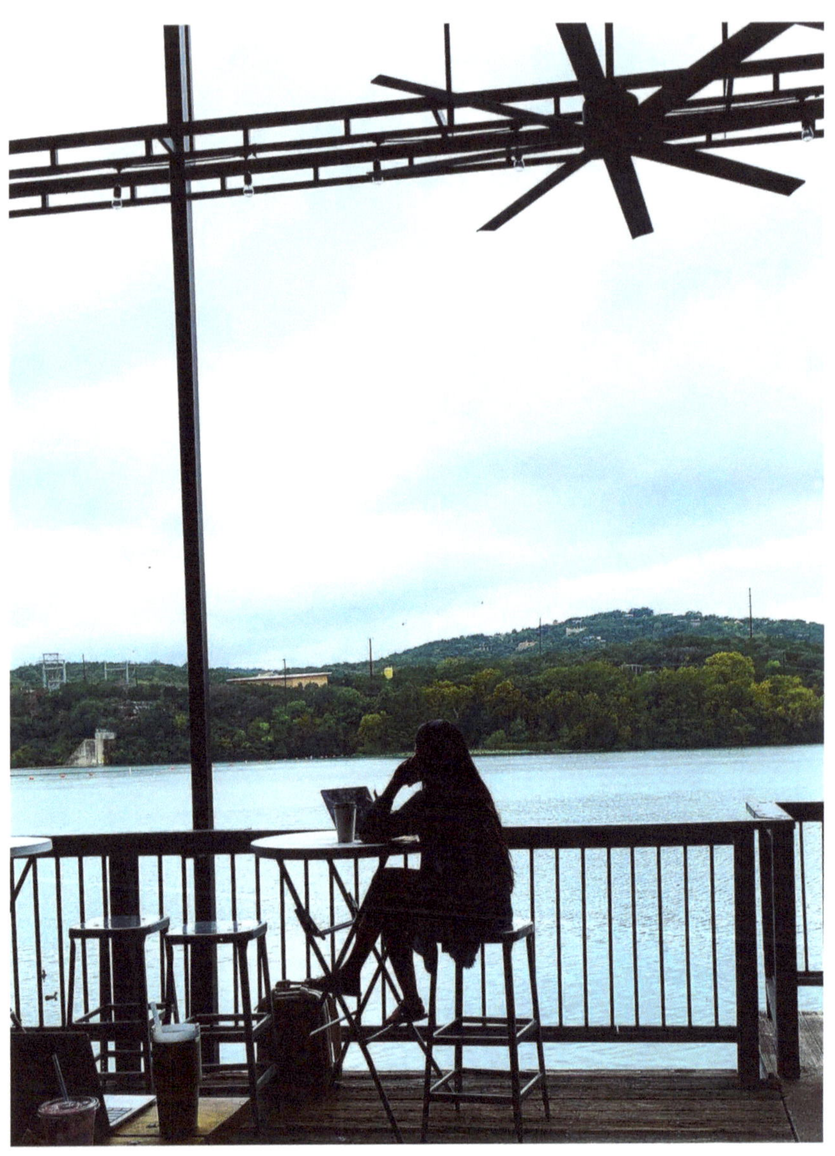

Saturday morning. Drinking coffee and listening to live music at Mozart's Coffee Roasters. The instrumental music rises above the chatter while Lake Austin spreads out serenely next to us, like a calm, blue blanket.

Austin is the "live music capital of the U.S.," but I'm overwhelmed by all the choices. Looking at the venues in the Austin Chronicle, I don't know where to start.

I decide to start small. Music in restaurants. Small bands at the Central Market. Mozart's Cafe.

Thirty minutes later, the line at Mozart's snakes out the front door. People come and go after drinking their coffee, and the music seems to fade into the background. There is scattered applause after each song, and I wonder how many people come for just the music.

Almost every table is taken, but it feels like an audience of three: myself and the couple sitting two tables in front of me. For some reason, this saddens me.

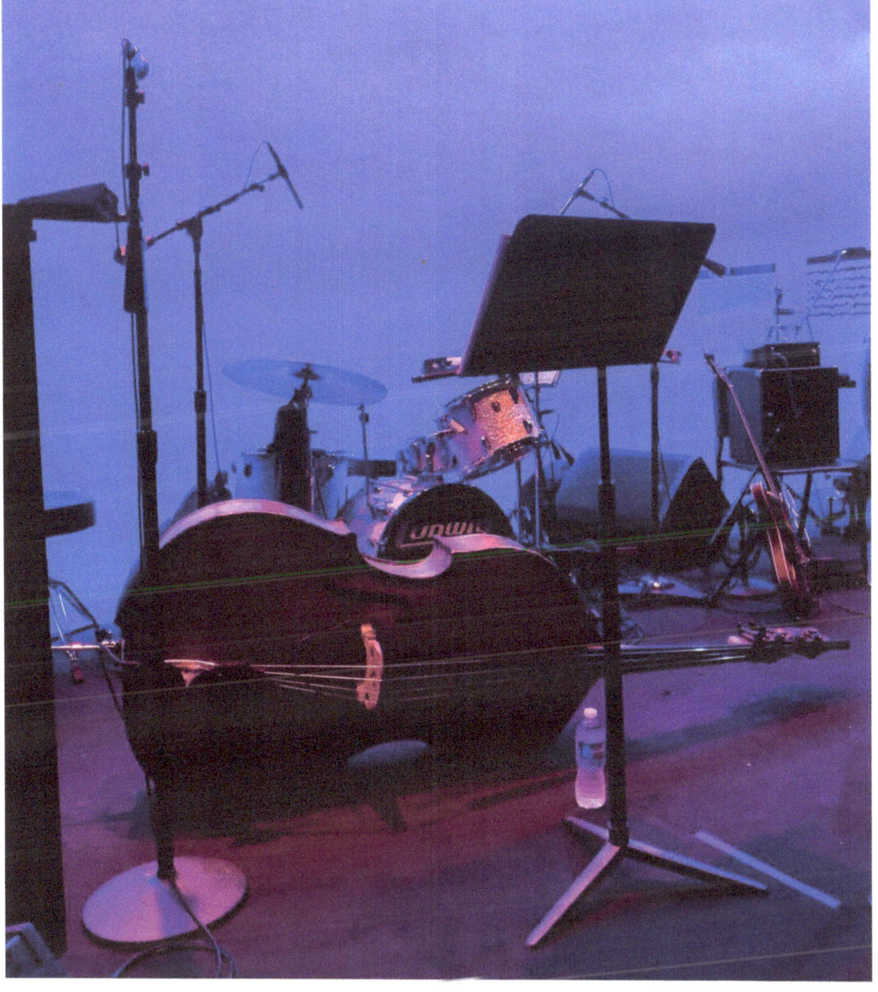

Later, I expand my choices. Antone's. The Long Center. The Paramount Theatre. I haven't made it to ACL or SXSW yet, but I try to make note of the musicians playing and create playlists of the ones I like.

While the small venues — the cafes, Central Market — may not provide the quality of musicians that larger venues offer, I still appreciate the intimacy of the spaces and the opportunities they provide musicians.

I'm also surprised to see musicians playing everywhere: in the lobby of hotels, at water parks, in the local libraries.

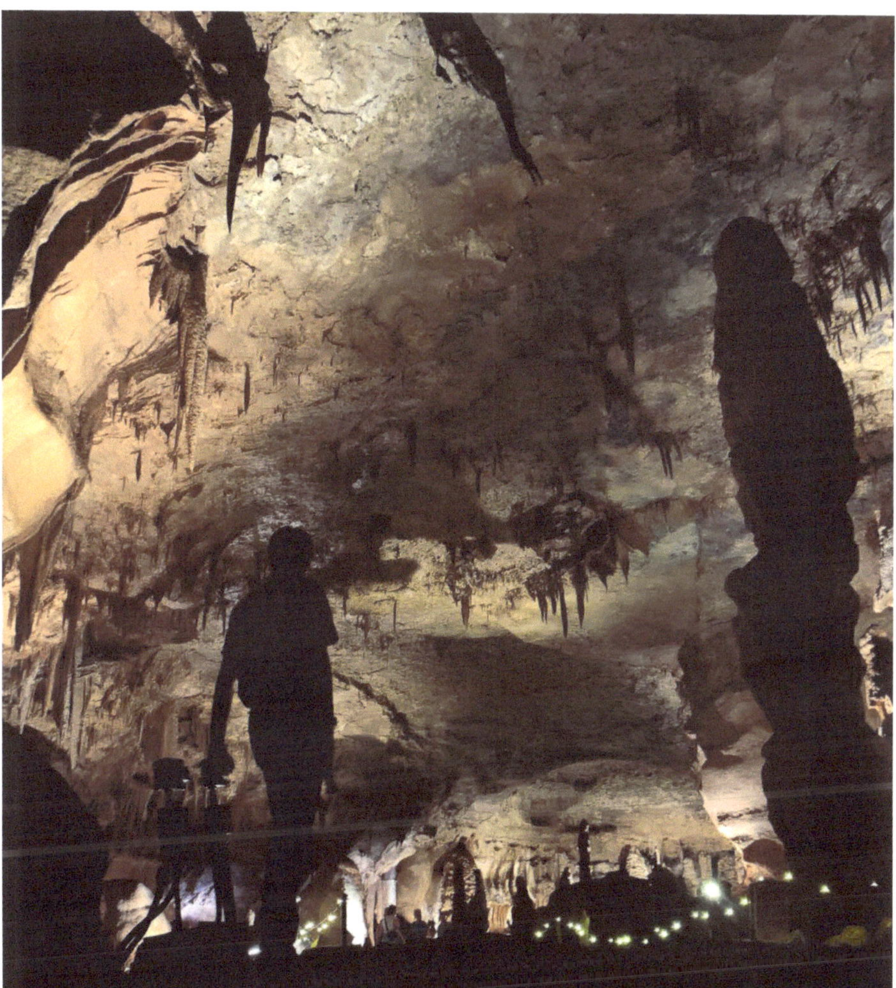

"Rural Texas" yields many surprises. I'm here to attend a concert in an underground cave that's fittingly called "Cave without a name."

When I get there, after 25 minutes of driving on a narrow road, I'm a little taken aback to find the cave borders the upper middle-class neighborhood of Boerne.

The divide between the suburbs and rural Texas feels murky. There are stretches of land punctuated by clusters of suburban houses.

I don't know why this throws me off. I suppose I have yet to shed my expectations about what "rural Texas" is and expect to see cows, wide swathes of land, horses, ranches, and gun shops (though I see plenty of all this, too).

I'm cheating, of course. A concert in a cavern in Boerne isn't quite the Austin music scene. In fact, Boerne is a suburb of San Antonio. But it's part of my discovery of Austin and its environs, so in some weird way, it fits.

It's raining the evening I set off for the concert. Or rather, the drizzle comes in fits and starts. This means we, the audience, end up with splotches of mud on our shoes and at the bottom of our pants, skirts, and dresses. I remind myself not to wear white next time. But, it's all part of the experience: climbing down 126 steps through rock stalactites, sitting in the center of a natural formation that has taken centuries to form, and listening to violins in a space that's perfect for acoustics.

It's a memorable night. In more ways than one.

By the time the concert ends, it's dark outside. "Cave without a name" is off highway 474, a rural highway that seems to stretch forever, until it abruptly connects with downtown Boerne at Esser Road.

There are no lights on the highway, so I hunch forward, hands tight on my steering wheel, driving at 10 miles below the speed limit. I can't see anything beyond my headlights.

A Texas Tribune article said that in 2021 "fatal crashes in rural areas accounted for 51% of Texas car fatalities," but only 10% of the state's population lives there.

That statistic makes sense now. The speed limit on these rural roads is uncomfortably high. And at night, visibility is low. Worse, the roads are narrow. I keep expecting to career off the edge of the road.

But I digress.

Living in Austin makes me curious about local musicians, whether it's Jake Farr at the Cactus Café, Soul Man Sam at the Continental Club, or the Black Pumas who soared to worldwide success and have a Grammy as proof. I'm eager to learn about what Austin musicians have to say and, more importantly, how they say it — simply because music is woven into every fabric of this city, like an ever-evolving song.

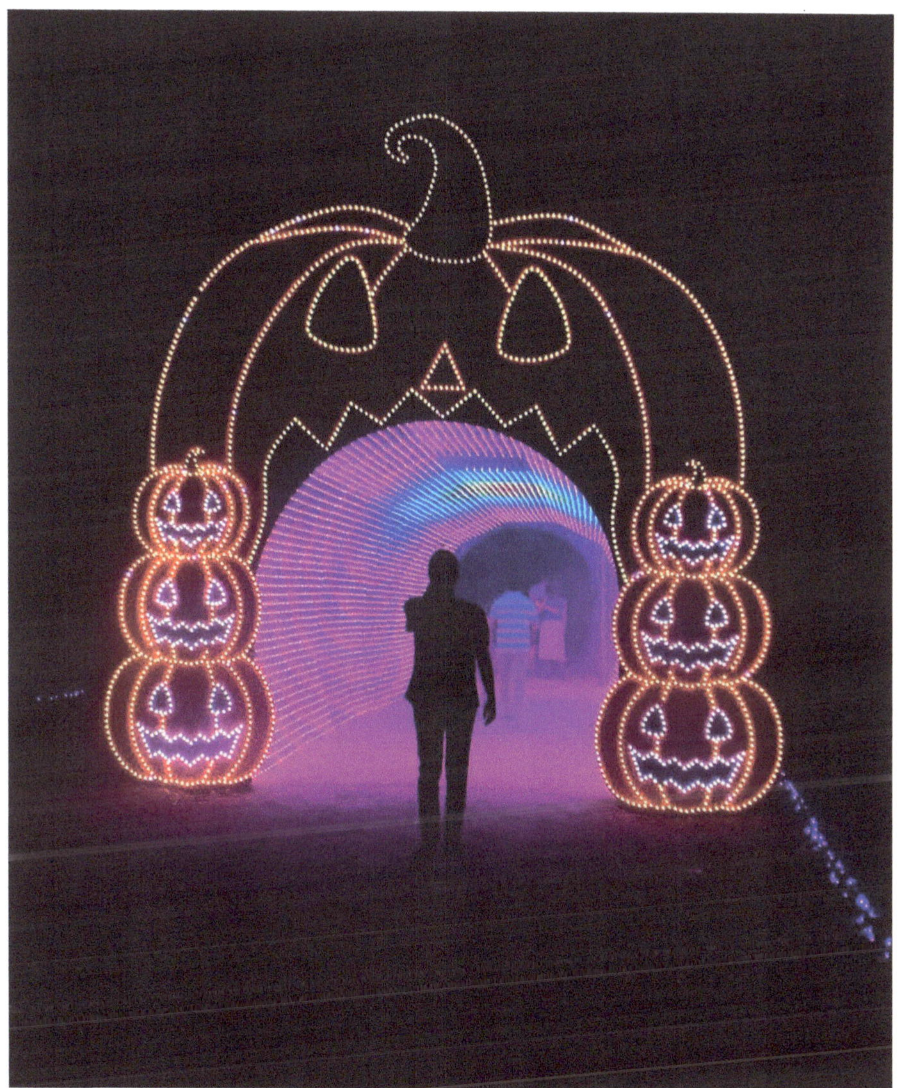

Pumpkin Nights

The mornings are cool, the afternoons are hot, and the evenings are comfortable. This is early October when I head out for my first experience at Pumpkin Nights. The half-mile walking trail full of creative lit-up Jack-o-lanterns, forbidden cities, and red forests is magical. Unexpectedly so.

When I buy my ticket for 8 p.m. on a Friday, I'm surprised how many nights are sold out (I would have preferred a Saturday). And when I arrive on the dusty, flat land at Pioneer Farms, parking at the end of Row H, I'm a little shocked to be behind crowds of people.

Pumpkin Nights in Austin gets bigger every year. And the crowds get larger.

I like this introduction to October/Fall/Halloween.

It draws me into an enchanted world of themed lands while reminding me of the pumpkin I have to put on my mailbox, the Halloween decorations I should put up soon, and the candy I eventually have to buy.

Austin's Creek Shows

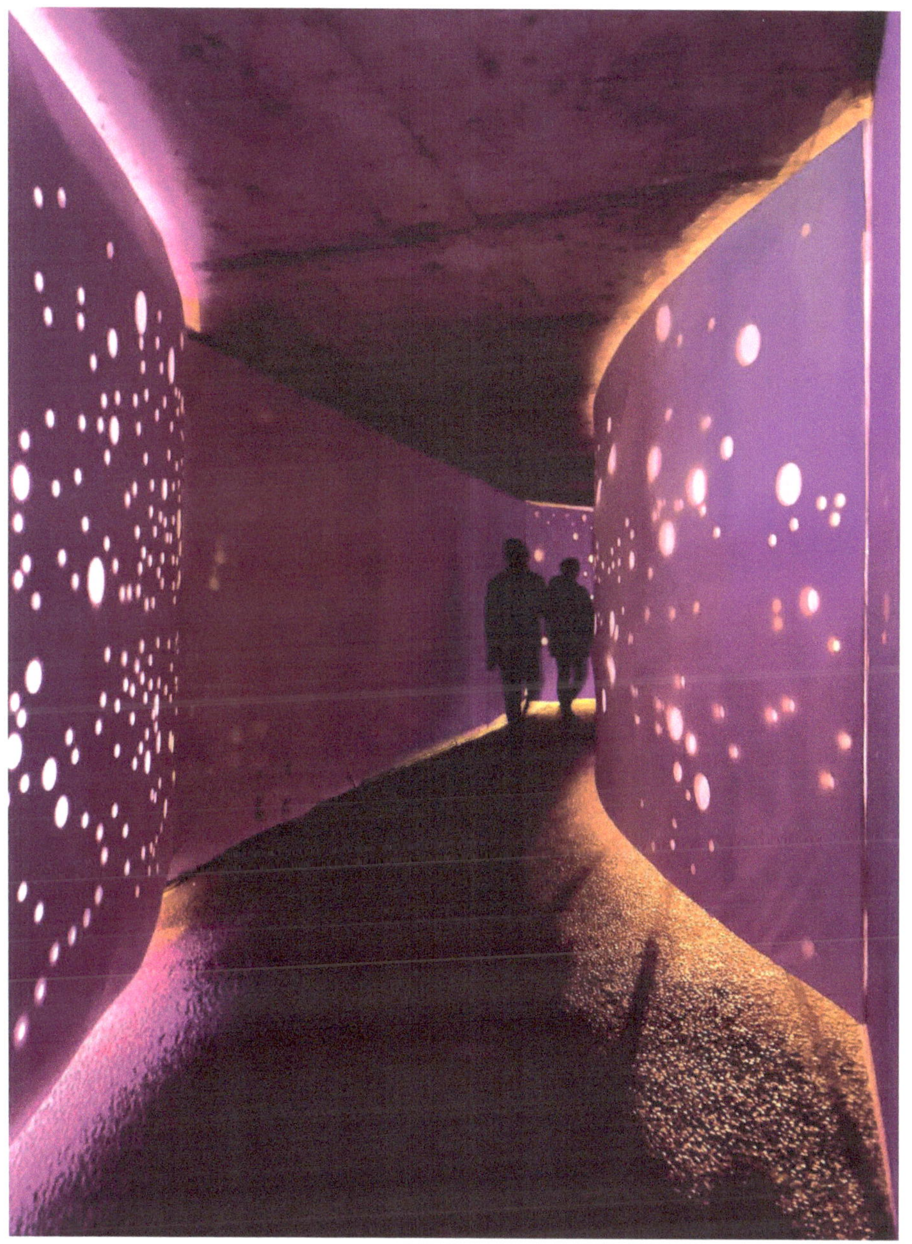

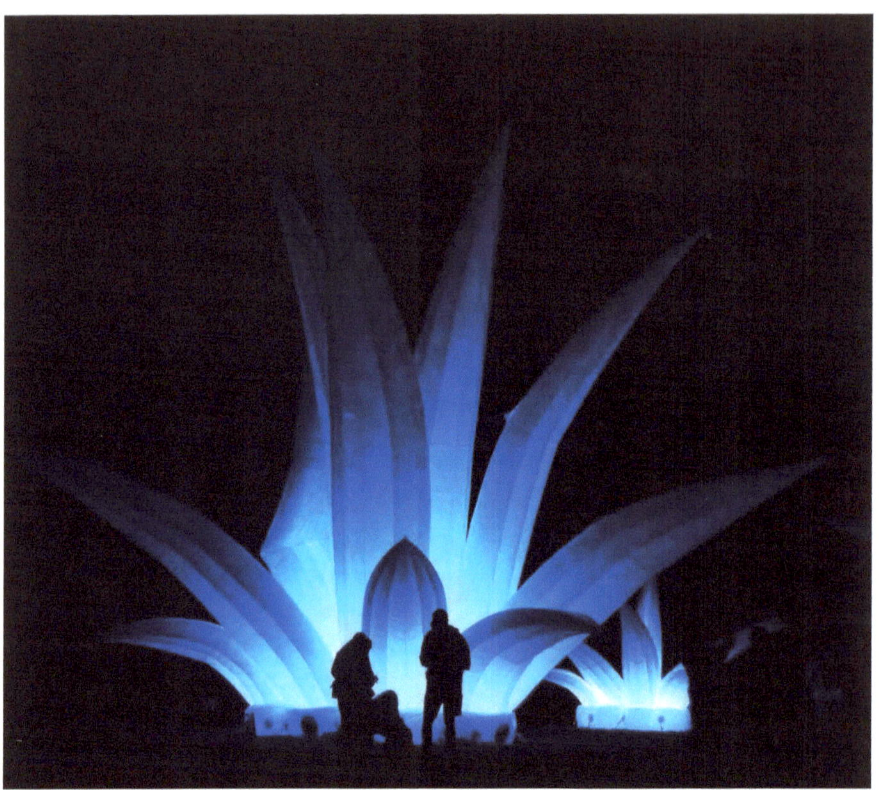

si-glo by dwg

I don't try to pin down what Austin is or what it's like. I can only write what it means to me. Everyone's journey through a city is unique, and really, often a reflection of their own life.

My mind drifts to the future. Randomly. I'm in another city, not Austin. But I'm a visitor here. Or I imagine I am. I point out where we lived, the restaurants we frequented, my running trails. I'm not sure who is standing next to me, but there's someone.

And then I imagine "when." What time of year should I visit? What event should I plan my visit around? The "when" is important, too. For some, it's SXSW. Or Formula 1. For me, it's the Waterloo Greenway Creek Show.

Austin's fine art scene is a little... lacking. But the city's illuminated light shows are special.

The first year, we're "late," intent on eating at a food truck first (it takes 45 minutes to order). The Creek Show is just a block away, but by the time we get there, my son instinctively turns away.

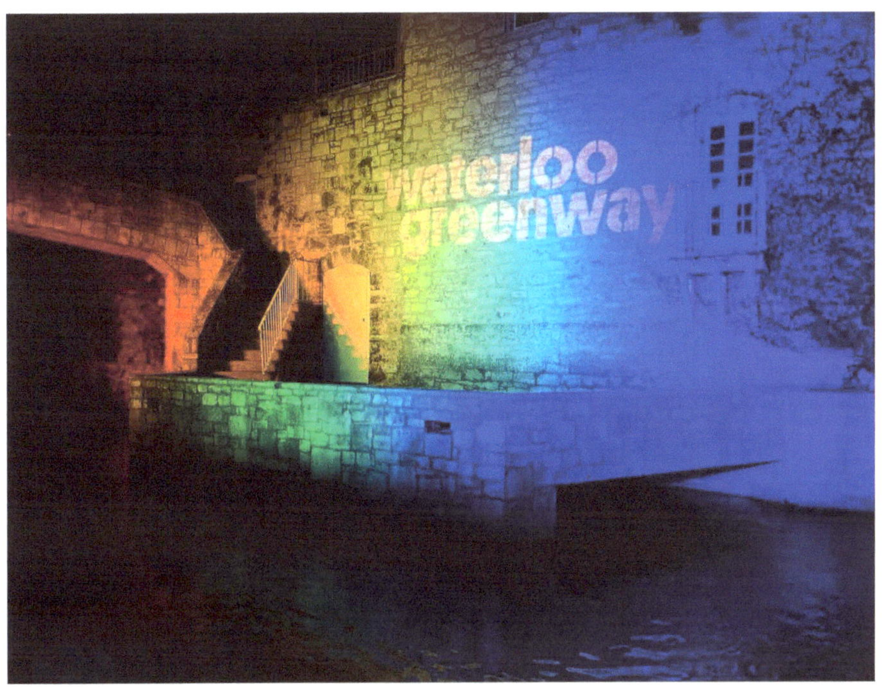

The line snakes and curls and seems endless.

I talk my son into staying. But his eyes dart in the opposite direction, towards the skyscrapers. He looks like he wants to make a run for it.

We were lucky that year. The line moved fast, and our "long wait" lasted only 15 minutes.

But every year the line gets longer.

As I write this, I'm scrolling through the Waterloo Greenway site, a little envious of those who have attended every show. The Creek Show started in 2014, and my first show was in 2019. I've missed five, and I almost mourn this fact.

I'm not sure why the Creek Show is special. Maybe because I'm aware of the work that goes into each installation. Or maybe it's simply the sense of awe I feel as the sun sets and illuminated designs light our path, beckoning us into a world of magical art.

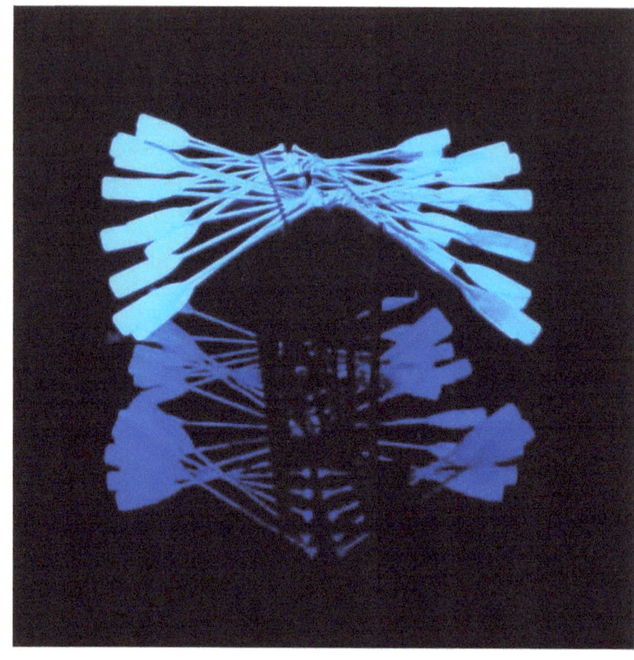

The Ghost Boat
Artists: Lindsay Abati, Johanna Spencer, Daniela Valle

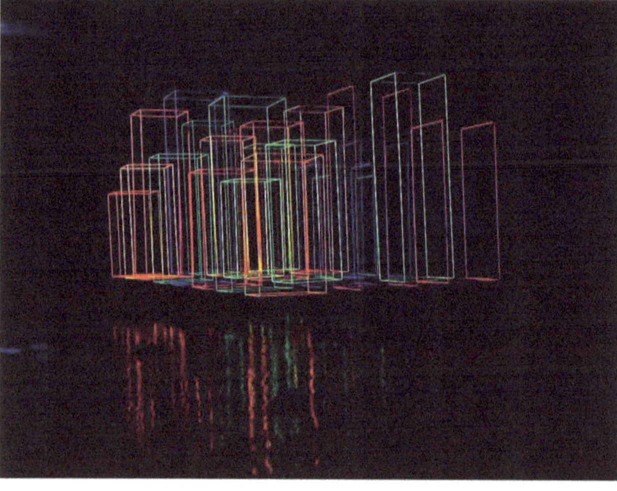

Neon City by AIA Austin

The last two years have been a disappointment, though. And after seeing three repeated light installations this year, I feel cheated — paying to see work I've seen before.

As I walk through repeat after repeat installation, I question if I'll return next year. Though I know I will.

Because it's an Austin tradition. Because I'm loyal. And because something new just might surprise me.

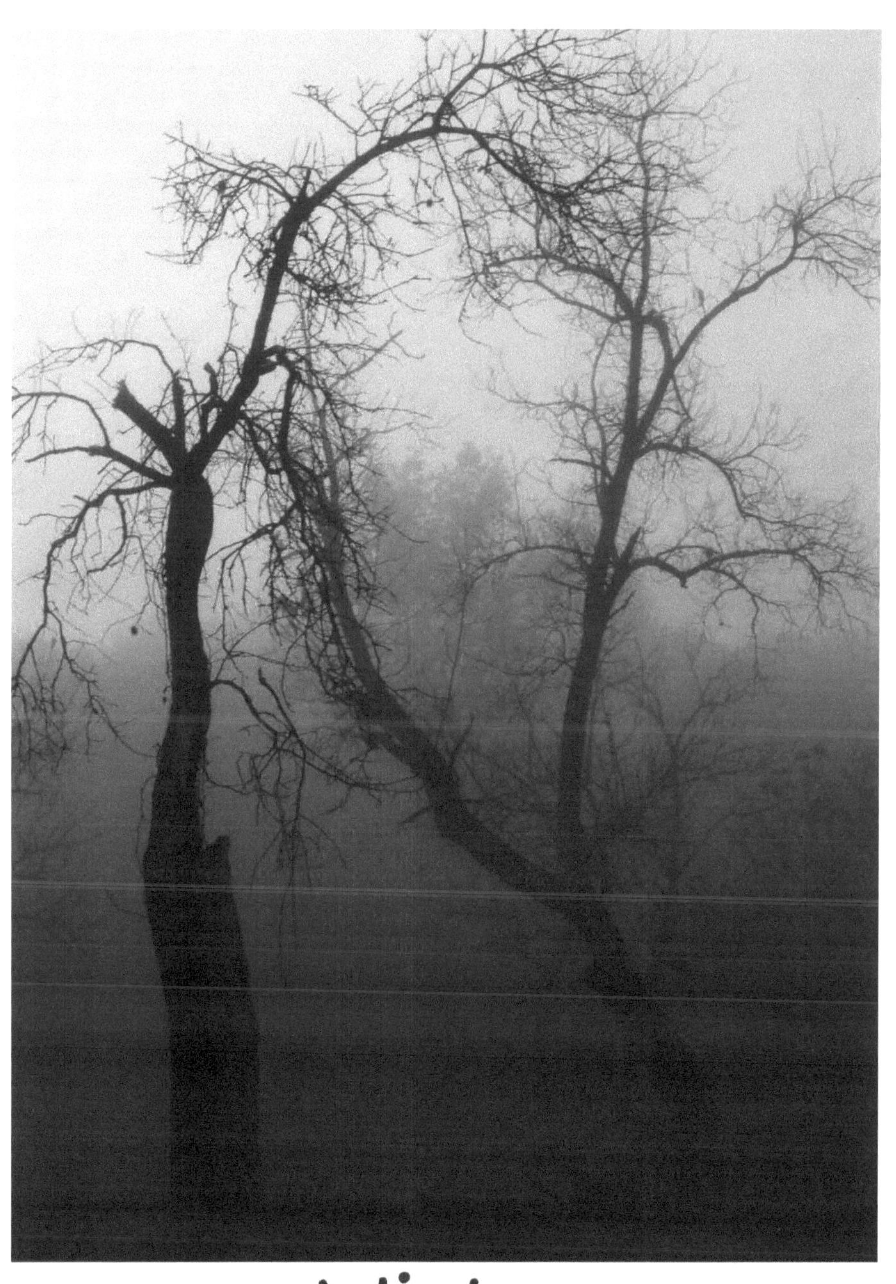

Winter

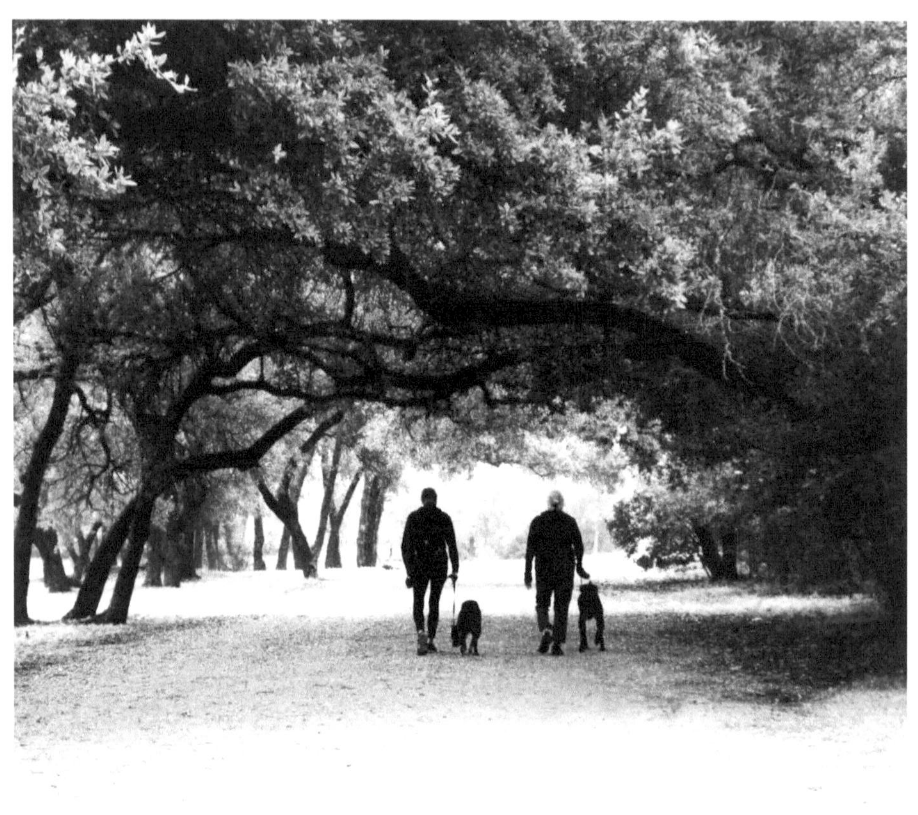

Winter feels deceiving, even gentle at first.
Fog.
Moody landscapes.
Skeletal trees posing for photos.

The pseudo cold pulls me into misty, picturesque landscapes.
It's cold, but manageable.
Even the light layer of snow has me fooled.

My son spends his day in the garden,
making a snowman
with friends

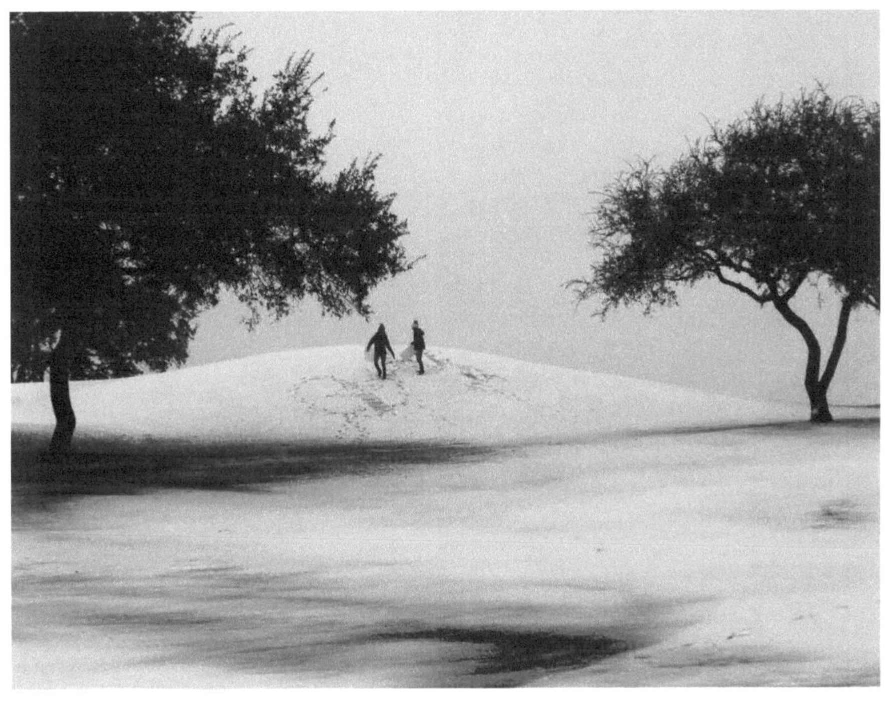

The deception feels complete.
We're happy with just a taste of winter,
like passing our hand over dry ice
without ever touching it and feeling the burn.
I spend a lot of time outdoors,
taking photos.

Then the winter storm hits.

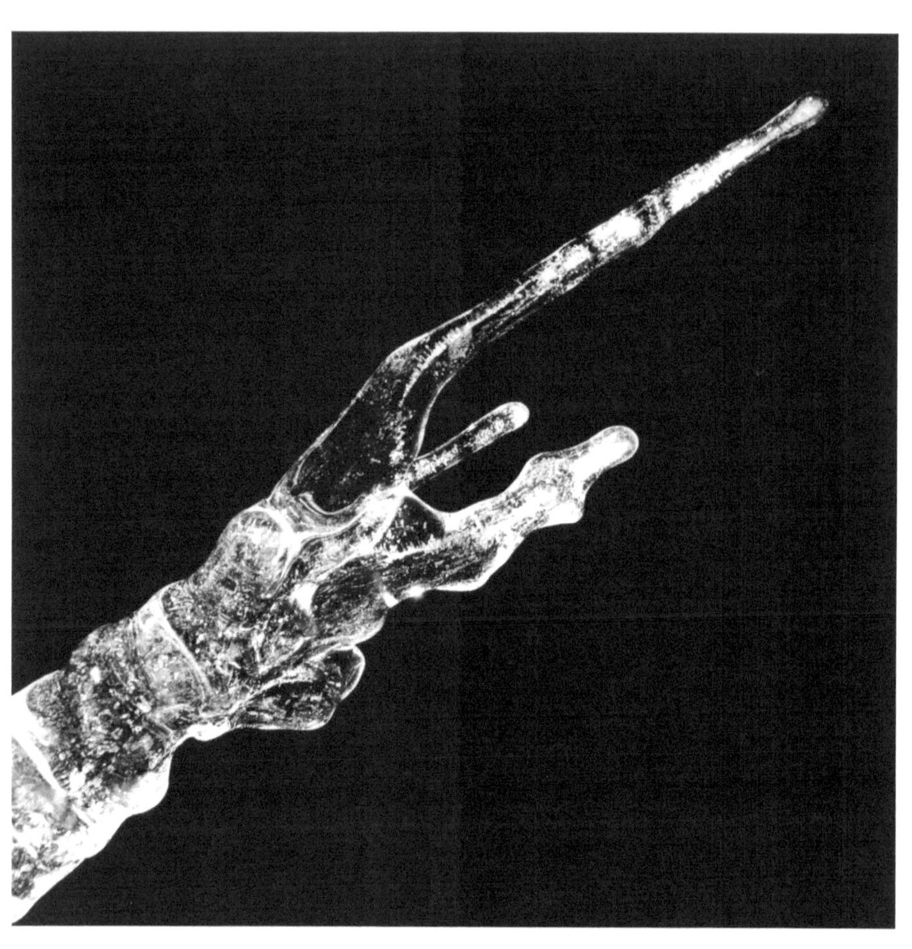

Winter Storm Uri

February 15th, 2021. Our electricity goes out at 5:15 pm. This isn't cause for panic, and I do what I always do when we lose electricity: I take my laptop to Starbucks.

An hour and a half later when I pull up to the house, the street is dark and our garage door won't open. The electricity is still out.

The temperature inside the house has dipped to mid-40's Fahrenheit, and worry sets in. I pull out our camping gear — sleeping bags, flashlights, lanterns — and we huddle in one bed underneath a pile of comforters and sleeping bags. Two adults and one child.

It's cold.

We sleep this way, cramped, for hours. But my husband slips out later — the bed's too crowded, he says.

The morning after, it's 30 degrees Fahrenheit inside. Outside, it's 10. This is the coldest weather Texas has had since 1989.

We have a gas stove, so we make tea, coffee, soups.

When the sun streams across the living room floor, we take notes from our dog and bathe in the sunlight where it feels 10 degrees warmer.

Austin Airport cancels all arrival and departure flights.

A day later, on February 16th, the electricity returns. Things seem normal for the rest of the day, and we revel in the fact that we now have indoor heat.

Later that afternoon, I receive a text. My neighbor. *Save as much water as you can*, she says. *We're going to lose water*. Water trickles out when I turn the faucets on, but I leave them running, filling up bottle after bottle.

My sleep that night is troubled.

February 17th. We wake up with no water.

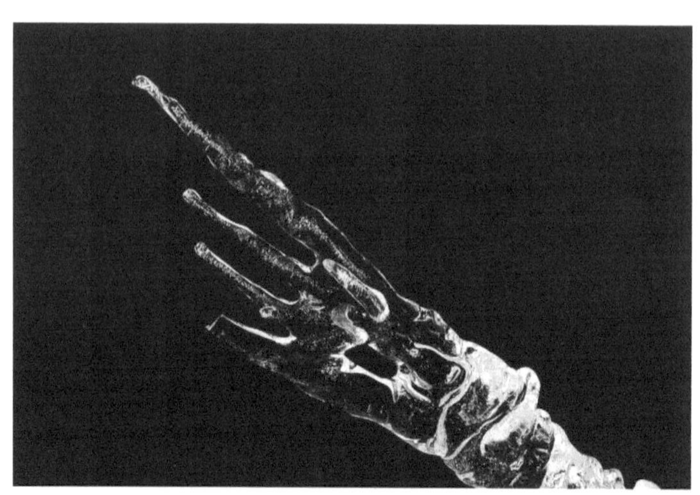

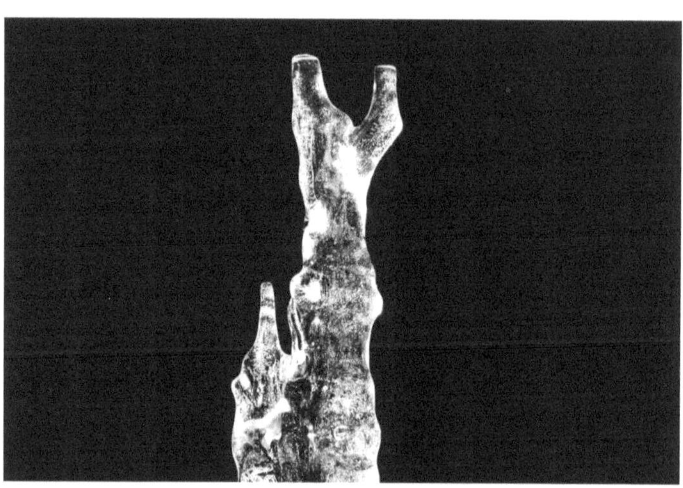

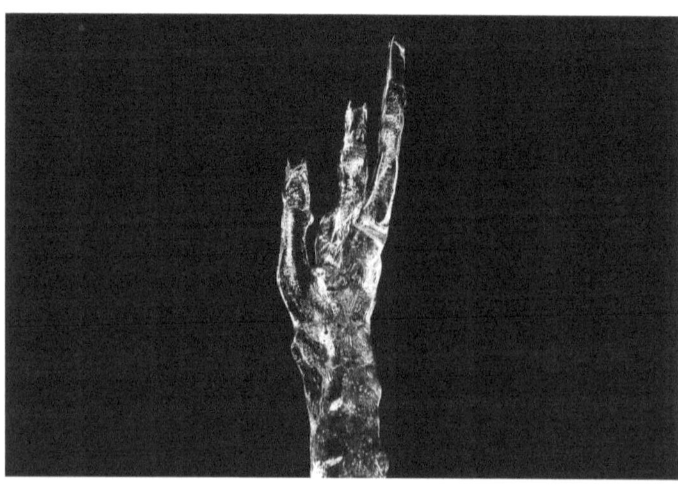

For dishes, I melt snow over our stove, but it's hard. I always run out of water halfway. Flushing the toilet becomes a chore. For each flush, we need two large pots of water: 45 minutes of collecting snow and melting it. I allow flushes only for number 2.

Our grocery store is out of water and is low on food supplies. The roads are too icy and therefore unsafe for the delivery trucks.

Meanwhile, our food supply is dwindling. So is our water supply. And with the snow piled high on the surrounding roads, we're effectively stranded.

Day 2 of no water. February 18th. I take inventory. We have enough water for 2 more days. I think. The days feel dreary, but we attempt a degree of normalcy. At least we have heat.

Day 3 of no water. February 19th. I email Austin friends and acquaintances. My son's school, or maybe a parent, sends out a mass email of a water pick-up spot. The city is handing out bottles of water. I feel a semblance of relief. We have 3 bottles of drinking water left.

Day 4 of no water. February 20th. My feet feel particularly dry, and I'm tired of melting snow. My shoulders visibly slump when someone in the house has to go to the bathroom for a number 2.

My outlook darkens. I work, melt snow, and take photos of the icicles I collect. Their skeletal features reflect my mood. I find them morbid and strangely beautiful.

The death toll in Austin rises to 28.

Later, the Community Impact newspaper publishes the damage:

— Percentage of Austin Energy customers who lost power   40%
— Traffic crashes   700+
— Calls placed to 311 for citywide services   105,977

Additional data goes up on the data.austintexas.gov site:

— Number of water line breaks in city pipelines   381
— Percentage of Austin residents who lost water for 2-7 days   50-60%
— Gallons of bulk water distributed to Austinites with no water   52,000
— Texas counties that were under a disaster declaration   254

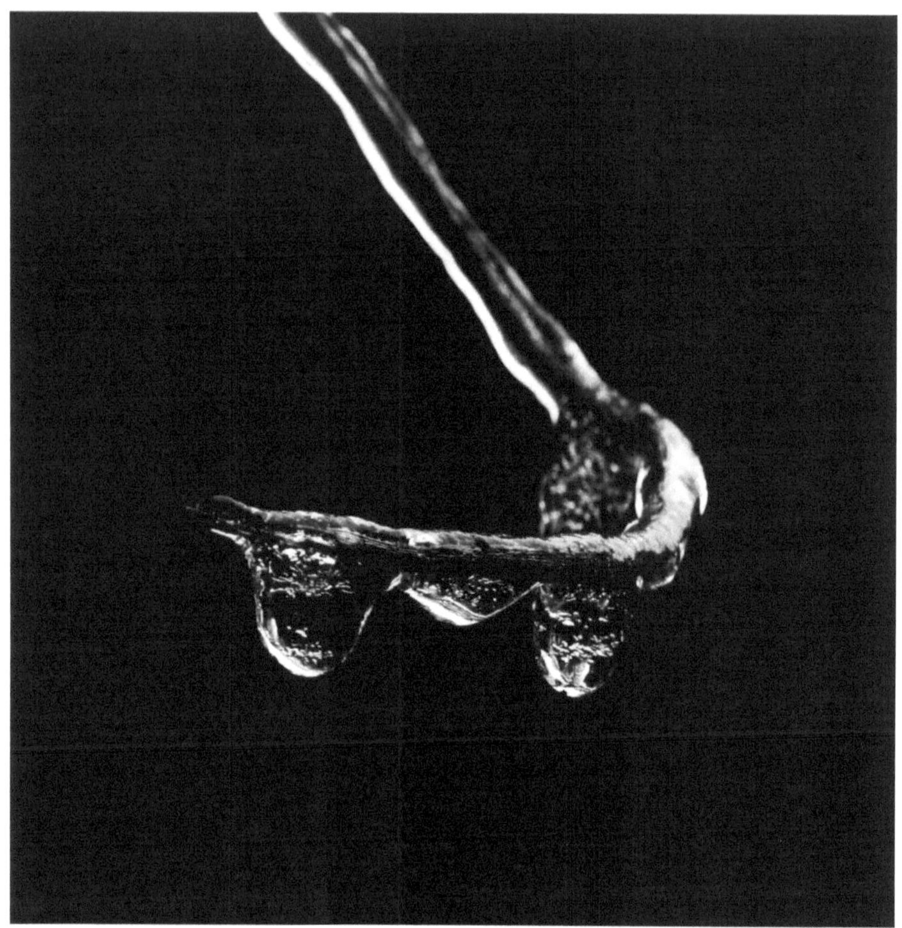

February 21st, our water is back on.

When our days feel "normal" again, I walk around the neighborhood, camera in hand, trying to find slivers of beauty.

One day without electricity and four days without water seem trivial now. But a year later, I buy a battery-powered generator and stock up on water and canned food.

Just in case.

The Ice Storm

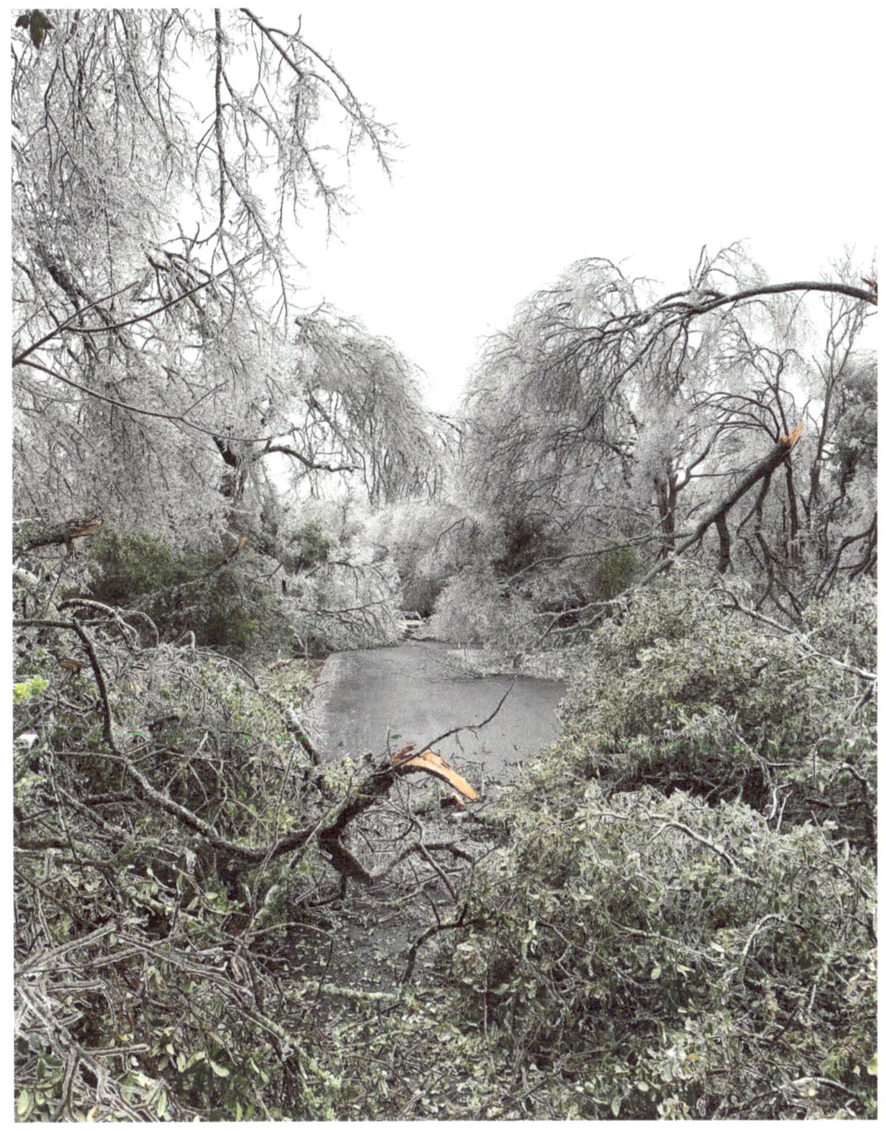

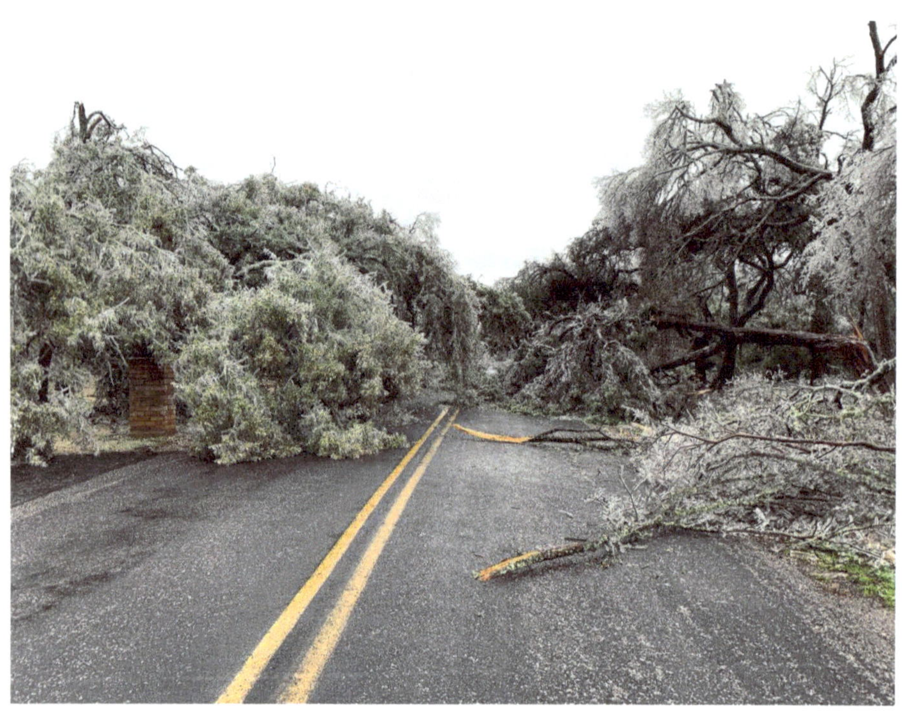

Two years later, in February of 2023, the ice storm hits, bringing beauty, then destruction. Schools close for 4 days (the roads are too icy for school buses), and we wait with bated breath. Fearful.

This time the trees get the brunt of the storm. Thirty percent, or 10.5 million, of the trees suffer damage.

I take photos of what feels like carnage – 80-year-old oak trees ripped apart like twigs. Their limbs litter the street, fall on parked cars, topple power lines.

We're one of the lucky ones this year. Our electricity remains intact. But hundreds or thousands of Austinites lose power. Again.

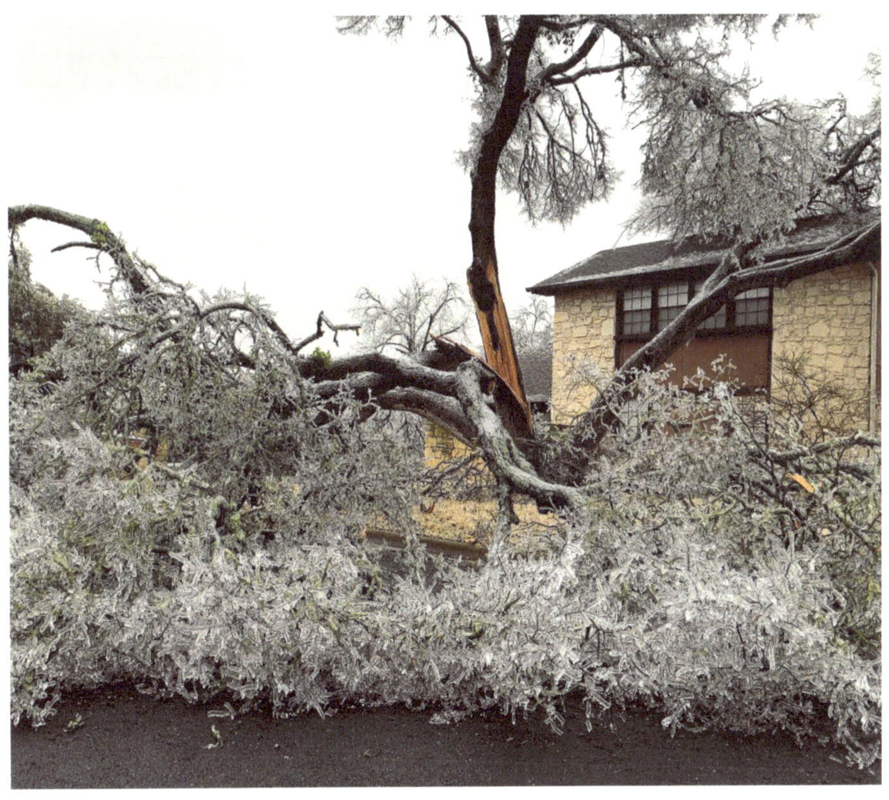

For days, as the ice melts, our neighborhood sounds like a war zone: loud cracks erupt randomly as tree branches break off and hit the ground.

A few blocks down, a woman stares at the wreckage in her front yard: an oak tree split in half, branches strewn everywhere.

I stand by her side as we silently stare at the mess, wondering how much money this will set her back.

Day after day, until the snow melts and the branches are cleared, I take photos of the destruction. Or the beauty. Or the beauty in the destruction.

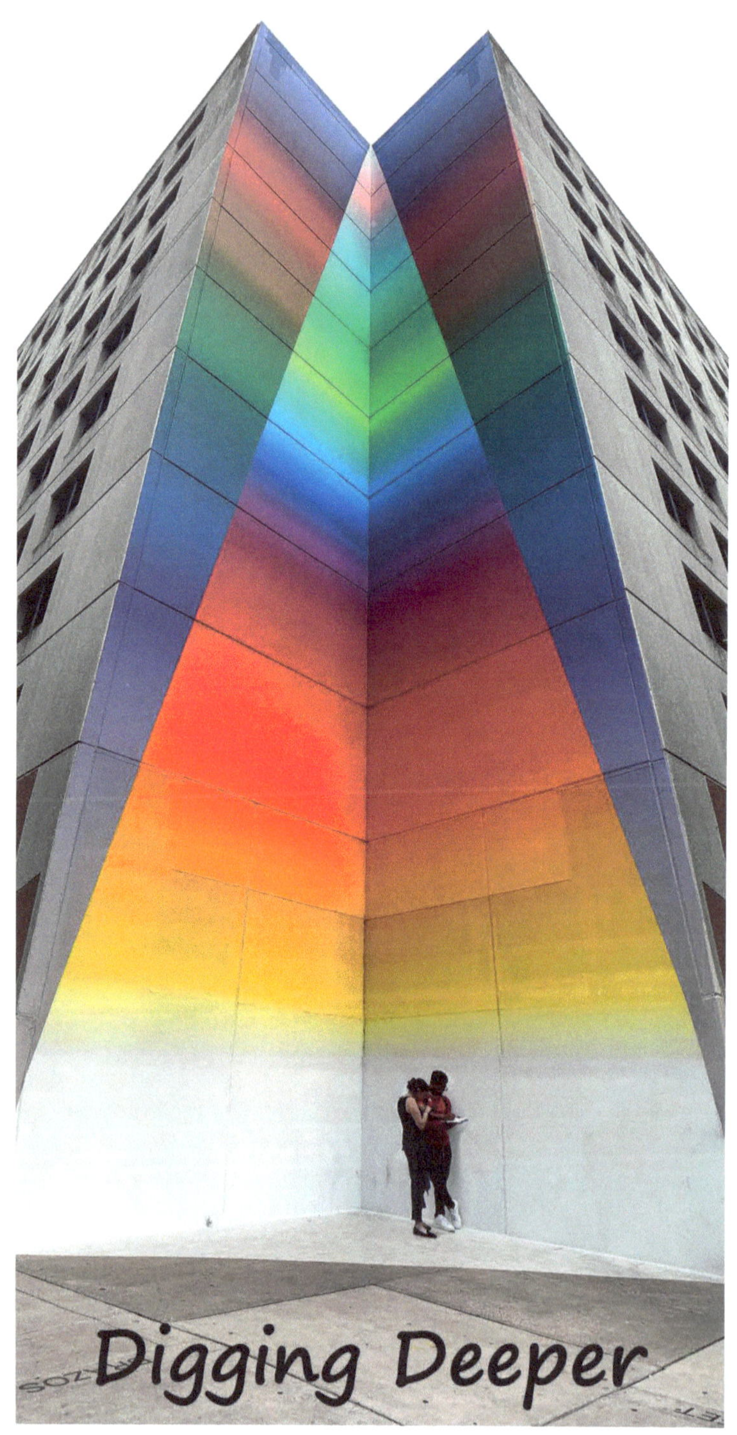

Digging Deeper

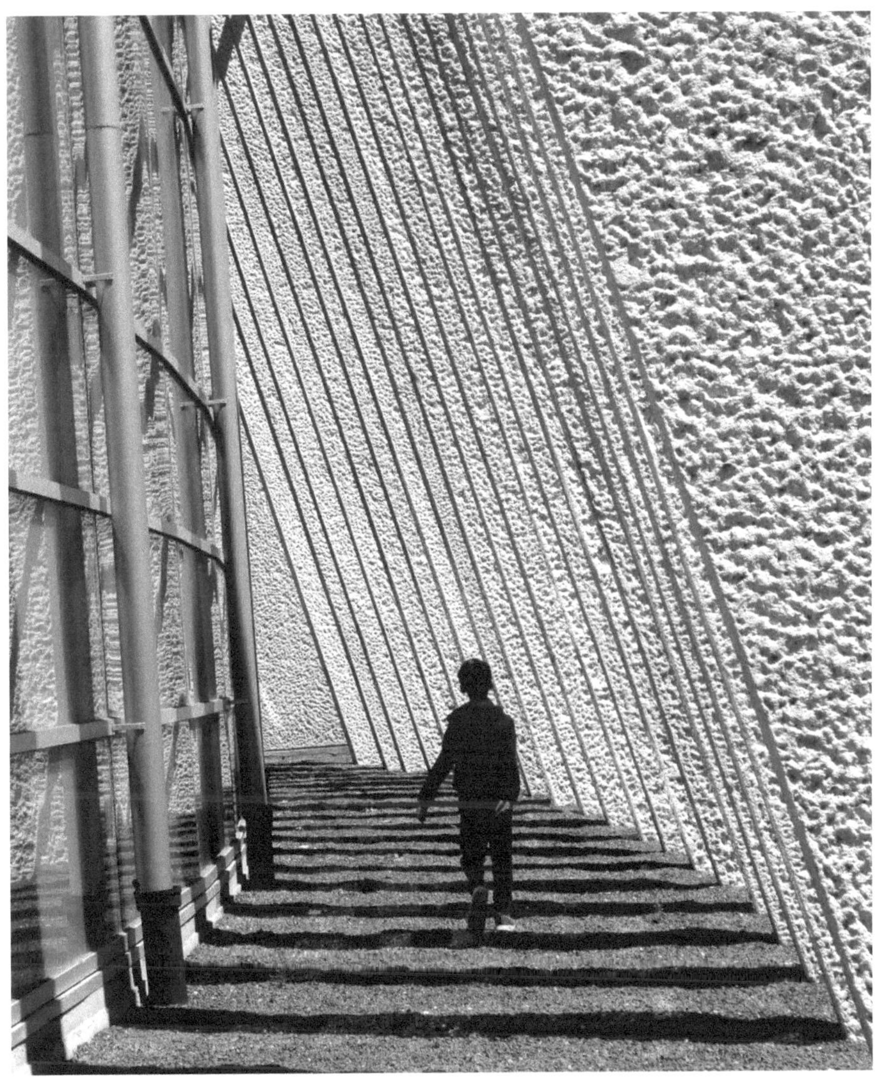

Emma S. Barrientos Mexican American Cultural Center

Discovering a city takes time. Years. Four seasons aren't enough. So I dig deeper, portioning off sections of Austin, discovering neighborhoods, one by one.

I'm learning not to rush things, to let things happen organically, sometimes accidentally.

There are places I stumble upon, drawn by the geometric streaks of light: the Emma S. Barrientos Mexican American Cultural Center.

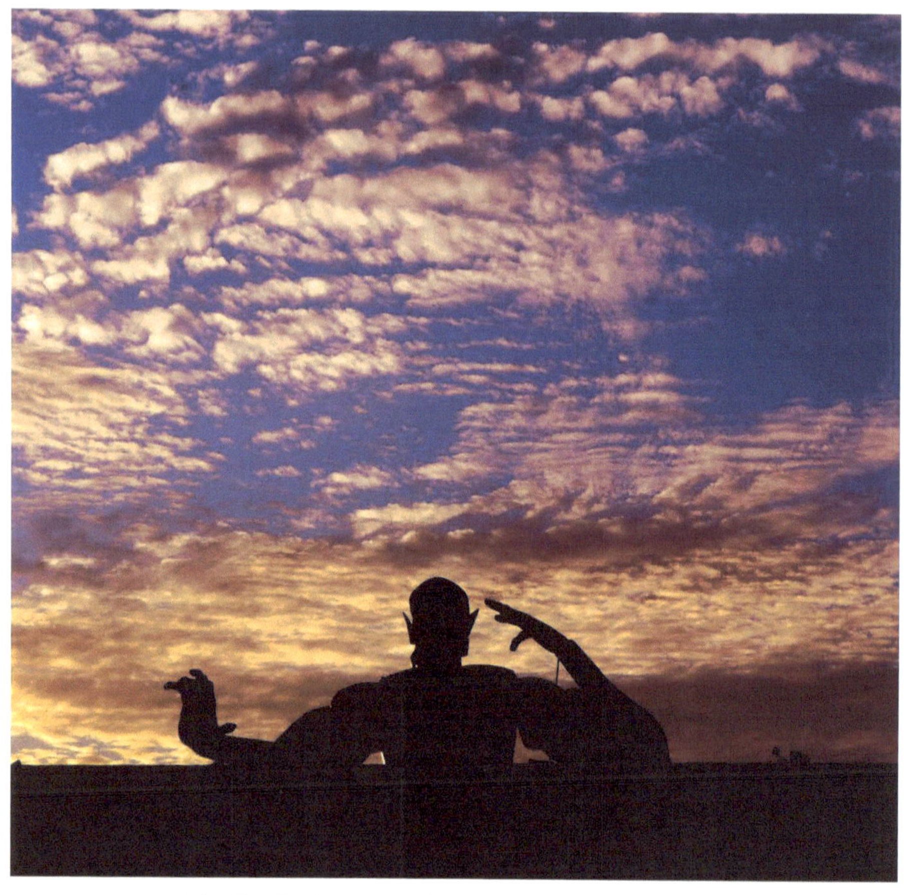

The Blue Genie on top of the Blue Genie Art Bazaar store

There are places I seek out, looking for a slice of rich black history: the George Washington Carver Museum.

And there are places that find me: the Blue Genie Art Bazaar, where I make it a point to "shop local" at least once a year.

On a day there's non-stop rain, I visit the George Washington Carver Museum. It's a small but impressive space, and I'm surprised — disappointed, really — that the museum isn't on any of Austin's tourists' lists.

There are three museums here that have taught me the most about Texas: the Texas Bullock Museum, the LBJ Museum, and this one. I appreciate their unflinching look at the state's violent past.

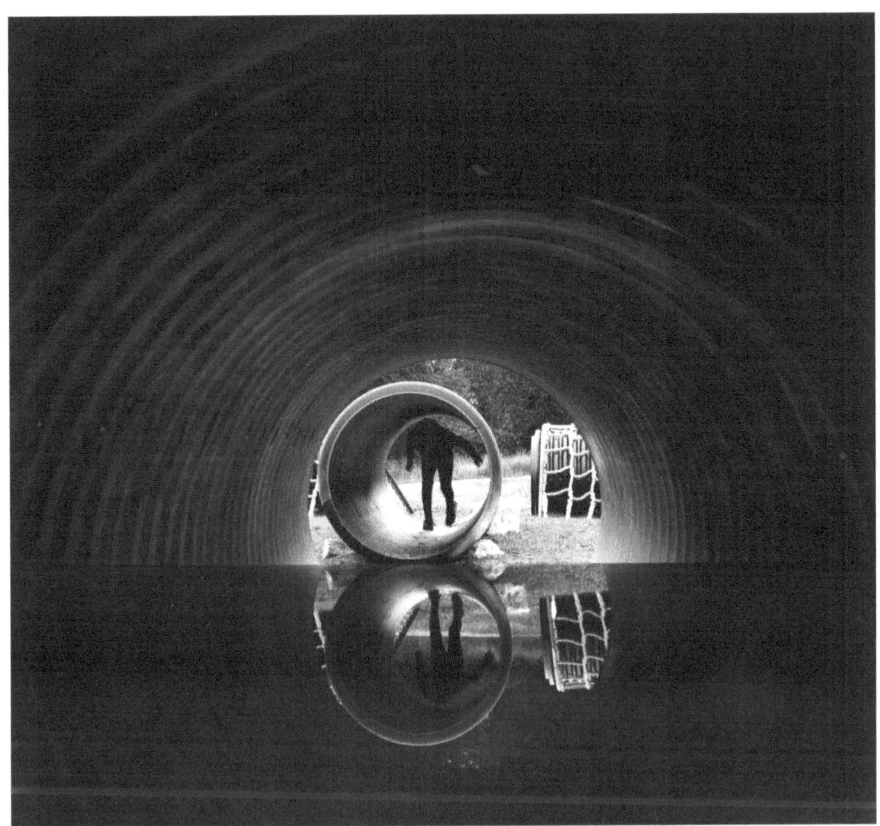

Fortlandia - Lady Bird Johnson Wildflower Center

But digging deeper into Austin isn't just about the places. It's about the people: the actress I meet when I see a play at the Ground Floor Theater, the artist I do a gig with at the Convention Center, the man with the white-striped suit who talks to me 10 minutes before the show at the Paramount Theater. They are Austinites, or have been for 15+ years. And they share what they like (or dislike) about the city.

As I return home after the play and subscribe to "Now Playing Austin," I'm struck by how little I have unearthed about this city. Five years in, and I've just scratched the surface.

Today, I talk to a fellow transplant, a man from Philly who's painting our house. He's been here 7 years. He misses home and specifically the delis in his Philly neighborhood.

I understand, but I can't relate. Maybe it's because I've lived on 3 continents (North America, Europe, Africa), so I've learned to find new things to love rather than long for what was.

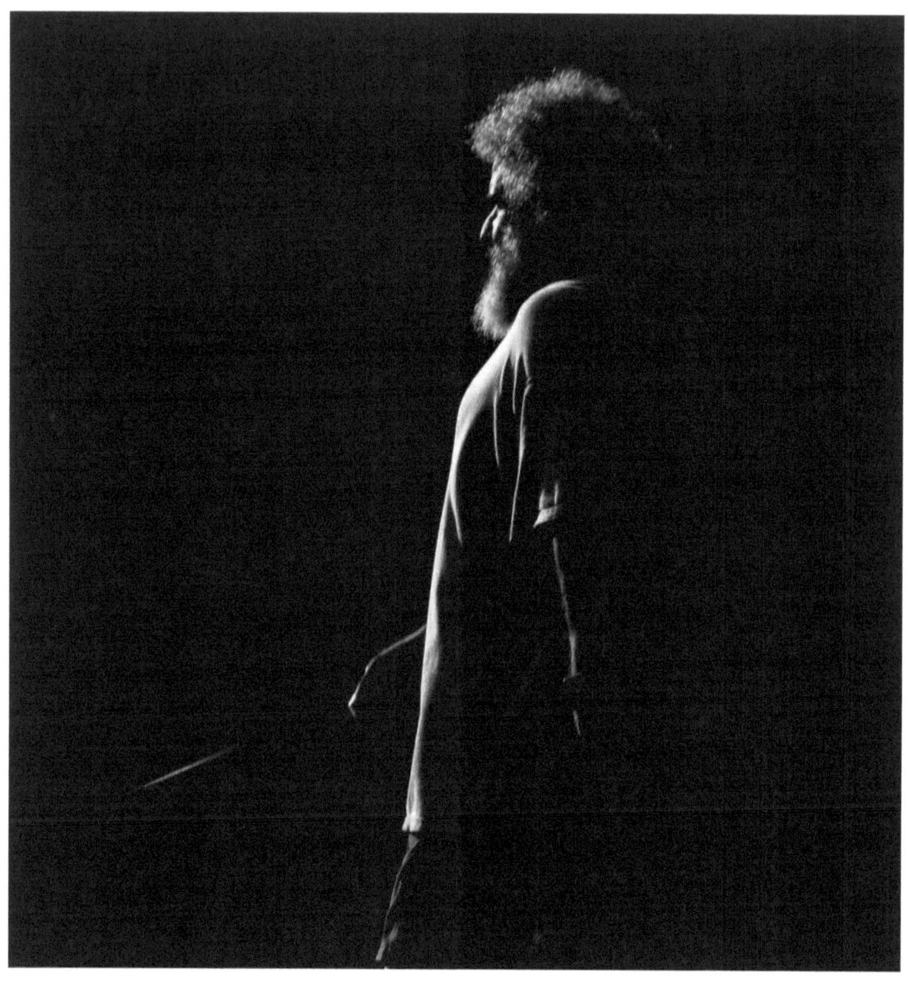

The strangers I cross paths with tell me a lot about Austin, but so do my neighbors.

Some, I know well enough to call friends. Others, I say a few words to while they're watering their garden or walking their dogs. For the rest, a wave is enough or a simple hello.

This evening, it's one of these neighbors who anchors me to this city. Before his annual Day of the Dead party, I'm in front of the mirror thinking, "I could use more. More makeup. More tattoos." This year, I put on face tattoos.

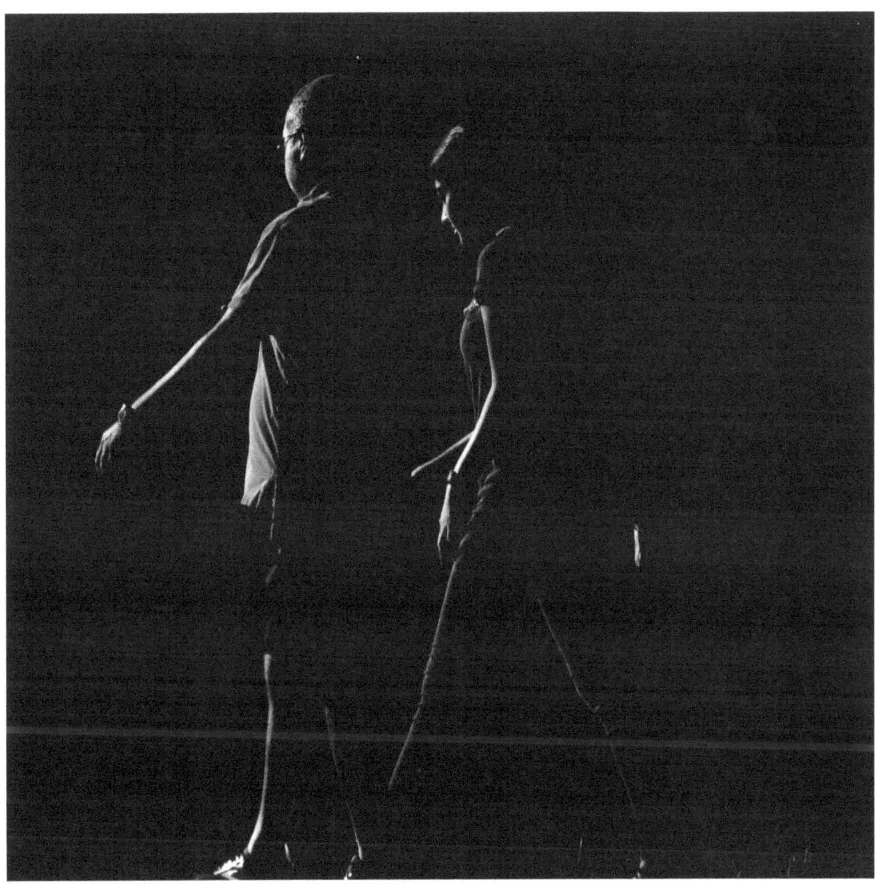

The weather is unusually warm, and the guests sit outside in the humid air as a full moon hangs over us. I always think I'll continue unfinished conversations I left dangling last year. Instead, I start new conversations with familiar faces or different ones.

9:30 p.m., we leave. It's still early, and the party will go on past midnight, the house's warm, yellow lights keeping the street alive for hours. Every year, I forget to tell my neighbor how much the party means to us.

"You're the spark of this street," my husband says at last as we head out. I nod, thinking: "The spark." Yes.

Spontaneous words that feel perfect.

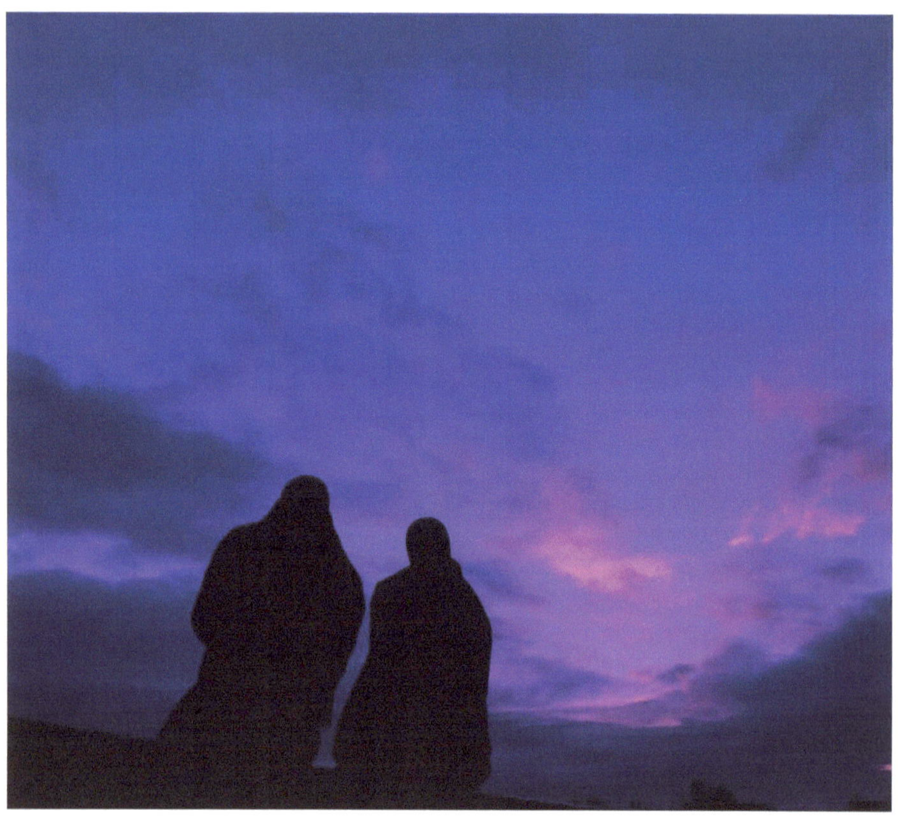

We're in the eye of the hurricane, though, and the neighbors on our street change every two to three years.

In a span of 4 years, or since 2020, Austinites need 80% more income to purchase a home. Mortgages and rent have almost doubled. A single parent whose daughter is in my son's class tells me she has had to move three times in six years because she can't keep up with the rent increases. A family on our street moved 45 minutes north to buy a house. Four years later, when the mortgages shot up, they sold their home and moved east.

People are constantly on the run from rising prices, so I'm acutely aware that these magical times – the feeling of knowing your neighbors for decades – won't last.

These moments, and maybe my life in Austin, are a little like watching a firefly's light glow in the dark, until it's gone.

Maybe that's the gift of days like this: not their permanence, but their fleeting connections and the knowledge that even with an ever-changing city, there are moments that remind us we were here together. At least for a little while.

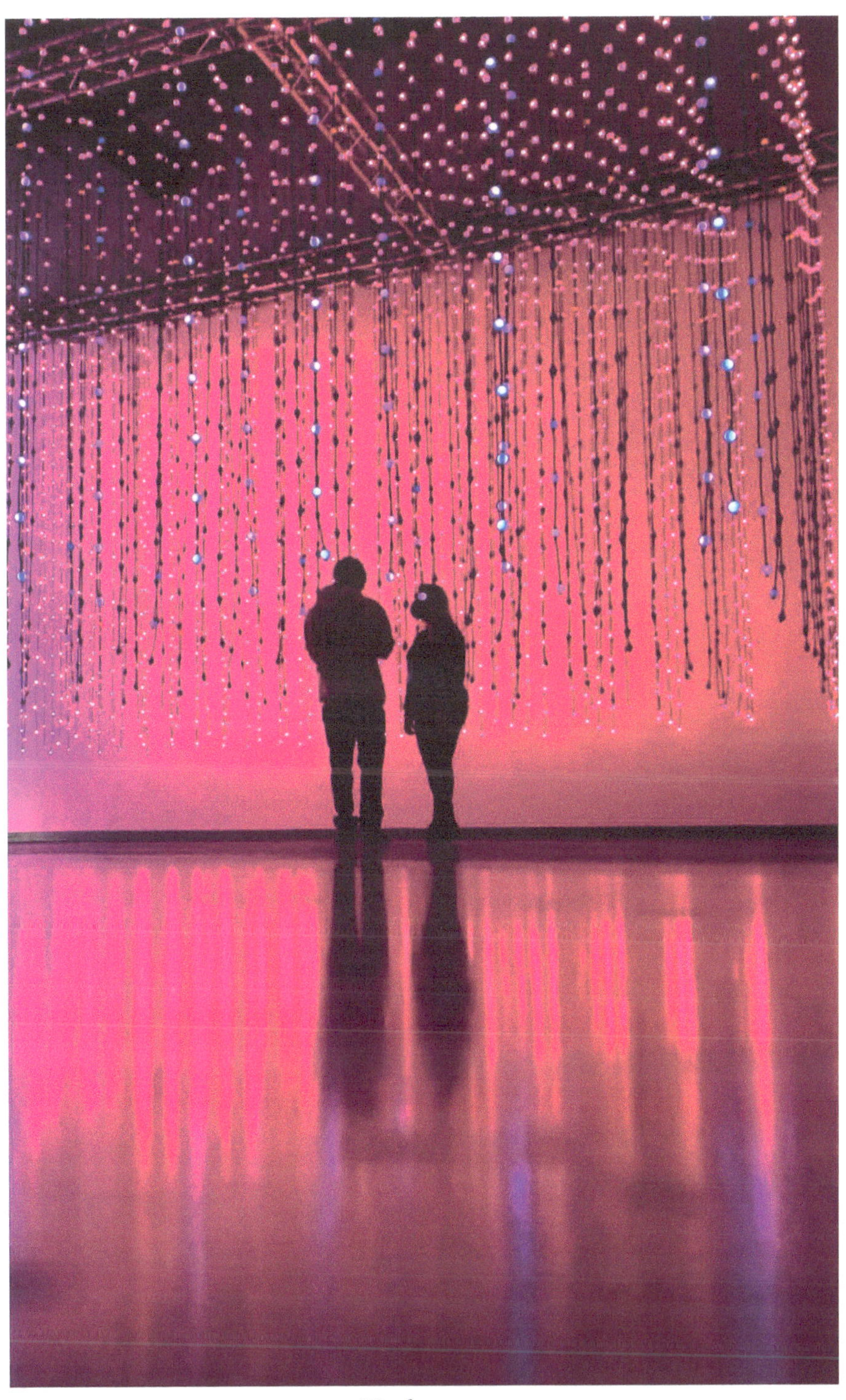

Wonderspaces

Cetywa Powell is a photographer and filmmaker.

Powell's photos have been featured in The New York Times, selected for National Geographic's Daily Dozen, and exhibited at the Museum of Flight in Seattle and the Grants Pass Museum of Art in Oregon.

Her documentary, *Santiago Files*, is streaming on Amazon and is available at select public libraries across the U.S.

See more at www.ten8photography.com